THE PANDEMIC MIDLIFE CRISIS

GEN X WOMEN ON THE BRINK

JESSICA SMOCK

STEPHANIE SPRENGER

HERSTORIES PROJECT LLC

CONTENTS

INTRODUCTION

STEPHANIE SPRENGER

March 13th, 2020:

I sit in a crowded auditorium, watching my eighth grader perform in the school musical, *The Lion King*. She has a solo, and our whole family is here on opening night with third-row center seats. During intermission, the crowd buzzes, asking each other, "Have you heard anything? Any messages from the district? Is anyone's Wi-Fi working in here?" We are all certain the announcement is imminent, and we are correct. I turn around and share with the strangers behind me: "The email just came through. It's official—schools are closing."

We aren't sure yet whether the three weekend performances are going to happen. (They don't.) Spring break is the last week of March, so we assume the kids will go back after that extra week off. (They don't.) When the play ends, the audience, armed with this new, albeit incomplete, knowledge, gives the kids a standing ovation that goes on and on and on. To be fair, the play was extraordinary, exceeding any expectations of middle school theatrical caliber, showcasing astonishing set designs, performances, and costumes. But as we stood and applauded our children, cheering on our feet for minute after minute, I think we also knew that they wouldn't be performing the show again, that their lives were about to change, and that it would be a very long time before we would be together like this again. With a lump in my throat and hot tears rolling down my cheeks, I felt grateful to be part of this preemptive community mourning, sharing grief we didn't even understand yet, for losses too great to comprehend.

September 13th, 2021:

I call my husband from the doctor's office. I try the words out loud for the first time, "I'm positive," and he is genuinely shocked, more surprised than I've ever heard him. I am the first to get tested, and over the next two days, the reality becomes clear: we have COVID. All four of us. My husband and I were vaccinated as early as possible, in the winter of 2020 thanks to our occupations, and our nearly-15-year-old followed suit on June 3rd. Nevertheless, we have COVID, and we aren't sure who Patient Zero was in our house or when and where we contracted it. It doesn't matter, I suppose. I frenetically retrace our steps, nonetheless.

For 18 months we were so cautious, masking everywhere, avoiding restaurants, Insta-carting our Costco orders, and moving all our social gatherings outside. We tiptoed into that beautiful and shockingly brief early summer era when mask mandates disappeared, 75% of our family was fully vaccinated, and, savoring the calm between the storms, we felt we could safely travel again. When Delta became a reality, maybe catching it should have felt inevitable, like it was just a matter of time. But it didn't—we were blindsided. Having a breakthrough case is demoralizing and discouraging, and every day I hope my vaccine will prevent me from becoming truly ill despite my asthma and history of pneumonia.

We put our lives on hold, again. Cancel work and school,

again. My fifth grader winds up with a fever of 102 the day after I get my positive test—her test 24 hours later confirms what we already know. She, too young to be vaccinated, also has COVID. She will miss Picture Day and the first two band practices and the first weeks of running club—none of that is important as long as she stays healthy, but what if she doesn't? She is embarrassed to tell her friends she has COVID, and I understand. It feels shameful. I only tell my closest friends and family.

I brace myself for another 10 days of quarantine, this time laced with fever/anxiety dreams about swimming with my clothes and shoes on, performing in concerts I am unprepared for, accidentally scheduling playdates even though we are sick, and being stalked by the characters from the Netflix show I'm bingeing. Nothing we are missing out on matters, as long as we can stay out of the hospital.

March 2020 upended most of our lives, in ways large and small. Some of us resigned ourselves to sharing home offices with now remotely working partners or worried about the safety of our "essential" spouses and family members; we cancelled trips, parties, milestone celebrations, and graduations. Many began working from home while attempting to facilitate remote learning for our children. Some lost loved ones, lost jobs, others battled COVID themselves. Zoom became the landscape for learning, teaching, and socializing; weddings and funerals were streamed on Facebook.

My co-editor Jessica Smock and I surveyed over 500 Gen X women about their experiences during the pandemic, and they had a lot to say. Gen X has a reputation for being the "forgotten" generation, the generation known for its apathy, cynicism, and stoicism. As we listened to the stories of our community members, a more complex picture of Gen X women emerged. While our collective vernacular expanded to include a host of COVID-related buzzwords—lockdown, masking, pods, social distancing, remote learning, variants, pivot, languishing, and of course, unprecedented—our community of Gen X women responded with their own list of words; anxious, overwhelmed, upheaval, surreal, exhausting, relentless, lonely, disorienting, rollercoaster, uncertainty.

Midlife brings its own unique vocabulary of challenges, with or without a pandemic. Many Gen X women have entered the "sandwich generation," balancing caring for children with caring for aging parents. Some midlife women have encountered a career crossroads, or are contemplating a second act. Others are newly divorced, re-entering the dating scene, or balancing life as a single parent. Motherhood at midlife takes a variety of shapes: starting a family in your 40s, raising toddlers, parenting teens, or entering the empty nest stage. Then there are the hormones, ranging from postpartum to perimenopause. Midlife can be messy under the best of conditions, but navigating it during a global health crisis is (we promise not to say "unprecedented," but . . .) another story. As Gen X women, we have found ourselves on the brink of so many things these past 18 months: crisis and reinvention, breakdowns and break-throughs.

The essays in this book feature diverse perspectives from women during the pandemic: they are mothers and daughters, teachers and advocates, wives and friends. Their stories highlight change, flexibility, isolation, connection, loss, and ingenuity, but at the core of each piece is resilience. These writers boldly and honestly chronicle their experiences of remaking their lives during lockdown, surviving remote learning (and teaching), grieving the loss of loved ones, coping with evolving careers and relationships, enduring a pandemic while caught between aging parents and older children, advocating for racial justice, and balancing the challenges and unexpected joys of the past year and a half.

In "Hugger," Anne Pinkerton confesses to her first hug during the pandemic, a masked embrace with her best friend, which she receives with "the desperate gratitude of someone who has been on a hunger strike and is suddenly presented with a juicy steak." Liz Alterman's essay, "The Parent Trap," explores the delicate balance of trying to emotionally support both her parents and her teenaged son amid their very different reactions to the pandemic. A love letter to Baltimore, Caroline Berger's "Both of These Things are True" chronicles pandemic life through the lens of working for a healthcare system in a city already suffering from the chronic ongoing traumas of community violence, racial disparities, and corruption, while finding moments of joy and hope for a better future. Laurel Hilton's story, "Little Earthquakes: When Friendships Fracture," is a reflection on maintaining the bond of deep friendship despite differing opinions on global health and political issues. In "Life Support," when author Suzanne Weerts finds herself having both a hot flash and a panic attack behind her mask in the frozen food section of the grocery store, she knows that COVID-19 is forcing her to reckon with not only her mortality, but also with what she's going to do with her life once her briefly empty nest empties out again.

This anthology is a rough draft of history and spans the earliest days of the pandemic into the spring that brought vaccines and hope alongside continuing uncertainty and division. As we cope with a new variant and enter into yet another wave of the unknown, it is our hope that within these essays, you'll find the comfort and connection of knowing you are not alone right now.

LUNCH BUS

KATHARINE STRANGE

Funny, I always thought if any disaster would upend my life, it would be The Cascadia Megaquake. After a *New Yorker* article anticipating the disaster went viral in 2015, with its jarring details of the ground beneath downtown Seattle being "liquified" and everything west of I-5 becoming "toast," I immediately began hoarding bottled water and house-hunting east of the freeway. Even after moving into a new townhouse a year later, I would occasionally envision how I could barricade the doors against gun-wielding marauders who would roam our post-apocalyptic earthquake reality, killing for canned goods.

But the end of normal came not with a bang, but in the midwestern cadence of my son's pre-K teacher asking me to clean out his cubby at pickup. When I only stared blankly at her, she said, "Didn't you hear? School is closing for two weeks."

And I laughed! Because Seattle Public Schools had vowed not to close—too many families relied on school for everything from childcare to meals to social services and even healthcare. As an uptight, overachieving PTA mom, I'd been arguing in all the relevant Facebook groups, attending (increasingly virtual) meetings, and had been reassured, again and again, that Seattle Public Schools would not close.

I am a self-reliant person. While my children were snacking that day, I retreated to my laptop, putting together self-directed checklists like I'd seen on Pinterest. Calmly, I explained to the kids that while they were home for these two weeks, Mommy and Daddy would be working. They could have unlimited screen time *after* they completed these 20 tasks, such as "build something" and "read for 20 minutes." I supplied them each with a plastic wind-up timer, the "20" circled in red permanent marker. We watched a Mo Willems Lunch Doodle on YouTube. Day one handled.

But of course, two weeks turned into four, which turned into a string of question marks scrawled across my calendar. My children didn't care about their checklists, lost one timer instantly, and broke the other. They would much rather wrestle and trash the house than "learn independently," despite my increasingly desperate pleading. They interrupted me constantly, making writing nearly impossible.

Isolated, I turned to Facebook to see how other parents were coping. It seemed everyone with means was "podding up," cashing in on unused garage space, hiring private tutors and/or nannies. Other parents (presumably those with yards) were decrying the children they'd spotted playing in parks. Meanwhile, many low-income families in my neighborhood who lacked adequate internet connections faced the sudden loss of childcare, meals, and social services. Everything was moving online, but not everyone would be able to access these things.

My family, neither wealthy enough to afford a yard nor poor enough to be shut out technologically, felt nonetheless forgotten. How could all the institutions we'd relied on—the schools, community centers, parks, and libraries, suddenly shut down? Why hadn't anyone sent me a *New Yorker* article about this?

Why hadn't anybody told me to hoard bleach wipes and hand sanitizer? I lay awake at night worrying about grocery shortages and how I would ever get any work done and remembering grim photos of mass graves. How had I never thought to prepare a contingency plan for a pandemic?

I tried to reassure myself that we were the lucky ones. My husband and I could work from home. We had an old laptop for our second-grader, a decent internet connection, and at least some communal yard in and among our complex's townhomes.

It was in this grassy space that my neighbor, Anadel, appeared late one morning. When we'd moved in three years earlier, I'd thought she and I were unlikely to become friends. Sure, Anadel was funny and easy to talk to, but the first few times we'd encountered each other she invited us on spontaneous trips to the library or the farmer's market. I had tried to befriend "spontaneous" parents in the past and it had never worked out. Their kids were awake while mine were sleeping. We were headed to the park but they hadn't eaten lunch yet. Spontaneous people required schedule adjustments, and being a primary caregiver to two young children while also attempting to write novels, that wasn't feasible for me.

Then the pandemic came along and blew all my careful plans to pieces.

When I saw Anadel outside, I commanded my children to power down their screens and practically dragged them out the front door. Standing six feet apart, I peppered her with questions about what she was doing for homeschool. She barked out a single laugh—"Ha!"—and gave a knowing shake of her head. Yes, she tried to get her kindergartner to use the school's recommended math website once a day. No, it wasn't working. Yes, they were doing an ungodly amount of screen time. No, she wasn't worried about it.

Standing in the spring sunshine talking to Anadel, I started to feel myself rejoining reality. I'd been connected to a near-constant stream of bleak news accompanied by social media brow-beating, but here, in this little patch of grass, things were okay. If Anadel wasn't freaking out, maybe I didn't need to either.

Anadel was good at getting her kids outside. One day that spring, a school bus driver spotted them on the lawn and offered them lunch. This was a new program from the district, and although our street was not part of any official route, the driver began to stop there every day, practically begging folks to take the leftover school lunches. I fell into a routine of working from six to eleven a.m., then dragging out my picnic blanket to eat district-supplied turkey sandwiches or bagels with Anadel and our kids. After weeks spent staring at screens, that patch of lawn was an oasis. Soon other neighborhood children began to join the socially distanced Lunch Bus queue, then some of our elderly Asian neighbors, who had been scared to venture out after instances of anti-Asian racism. None of these others joined our pandemic bubble, but it was comforting to see that we were all still here, all eating the same industrially cut carrot coins in our respective homes.

Our lunch routine got us through a summer without day camp, swimming, or spray parks. When I found out that my youngest would not get a chance at "normal" kindergarten, Anadel was there to listen. Every day she was there, standing barefoot on the sidewalk, watering her tomatoes, a beacon of normalcy.

It was against HOA rules, but I added an inflatable pool to the communal yard. Our kids splashed and yelled. None of the neighbors complained, even when it killed a patch of grass. In those hot, relentless days, it seemed everyone had found a little flexibility.

Neighborly sympathy even quelled the normal fundraising

competition between area PTAs. In south Seattle, ten such groups combined to apply for emergency grant funding to help our community's neediest families. The wealthier schools in our coalition made sure that those of us from poorer schools got the lion's share of the funding, and my school was able to distribute almost $30,000 to needy families. We paid internet bills and bought grocery gift cards. We paid for childcare and emergency dental work, countless bus passes, and helped fund repair on a busted transmission.

These are the images I will take with me from our pandemic year: school staff standing in a baking parking lot to hand out laptops and school supplies, chefs packaging up free meal kits for hungry families, essential workers who showed up day in and day out despite the risks. It was my neighbor, Amy, who brought me a 25-pound sack of flour from Costco so I could bake my special Easter bread. It was my fellow Seattleites who took the maxim to "flatten the curve" so seriously that we never exceeded our ICU capacity, despite having the nation's first outbreak. And I will think of Anadel, who listened to countless meltdowns, and even had a few of her own. My community gave me faith when I had none left.

The megaquake no longer keeps me up at night. When I think of it now, I don't imagine guns and anarchy, but a Lunch Bus creeping up the broken pavement, dishing up turkey sandwiches and hope.

HUGGER

ANNE PINKERTON

It was six whole months into the pandemic before my best friend finally, spontaneously, hugged me.

It's not that I hadn't seen her all that time. We had taken at least a dozen strolls in a variety of lovely outdoor spots, drunk cocktails sitting far apart in her back garden, sat chatting in the open doors of our cars in a parking lot, and had more Zoom dates than I could count during the long season of COVID-19. But we hadn't made physical contact in all that time. Not even an elbow bump or pat on the back. Though her pandemic puppy had licked my face, nibbled my wrists, and jumped in my lap, I hadn't touched her mom, my dear friend, for half a year.

On a late Sunday morning, after we took a long walk around a beautiful local lake, talking about life and love and nature, Karen just grabbed me. My arms flew around her with the desperate gratitude of someone who had been on a hunger strike for weeks and was suddenly presented with a juicy steak.

"I couldn't help it!" she said, and my heart heaved.

"I'm so glad," I whispered right into her ear, relaxing into her body as tears spontaneously formed in my eyes.

We had resisted for so long, out of an abiding sense of

responsibility—to ourselves, to our partners, to the community at large—and out of real fear of the dangerous invisible stranger that had entered our midst. Karen and I were both masked for our embrace, but the event felt like a crime anyway. I looked around nervously, wondering whether any passers-by were witnesses.

Holding my chosen sister in my arms at last, I lingered long, the feel of her delicate shoulder blades under my palms, her warm torso in my grasp, her fine hair just barely grazing my temple. I knew it would be some time until I held her again, so I tried to memorize the feeling. Karen is my only friend smaller than me—I'm only five foot two myself—and when I hug her, I feel protective in my ability to envelop her frame.

A WRITING GROUP facilitator once asked me at the end of a session whether I was "a huggable kind of person." She had no idea.

Hugs are my favorite. So much so that some friends find it a little *much*. Some colleagues who have become friends definitely do—and it's tricky to know the right boundaries when you really enjoy connecting with others through hugging. But I've learned to ask questions before getting too grabby; it's only appropriate, and I know it. "Would you like a hug?" or "Can I give you a hug?" are in my back pocket after a couple of stiff receptions to my squeezes. I try—sometimes unsuccessfully—not to feel rejected by a "No."

There is no touch I love as universally as a hug. It works for lovers, best friends, colleagues, family members, and little kids who are feeling blue. Being wrapped in the arms of someone and wrapping them in mine is my definition of comfort and contentment. I might go so far as to say hugs are the thing that makes me feel most safe.

WHEN THE LOCKDOWNS began in early 2020, a friend on social media posed the question, "What do you miss most?" As you can imagine, my answer was automatic.

Such a wholesome and warm kind of contact, the hug. I never imagined a day in which holding someone affectionately could, by itself, be dangerous. It helped me to know that others are just as hug-obsessed as I am and have been looking for creative solutions. It only took a month or so of isolation for grandkids to figure out ways to hug their grandparents through plastic sheeting and for *The New York Times* to publish an article with elaborate tips on how to hug safely. For someone who went through puberty during the AIDS epidemic, the notion that a simple clothed embrace might kill was stunning, so I simply didn't risk it.

THIS IS why I was extra appreciative that, on that Sunday morning, Karen took the initiative. She had been even more nervous about the virus than I. So, it was almost like dating, waiting for the other party to make the first move, and being so psyched when they did.

Immediately upon arriving home, I confessionally blurted to my husband, "I hugged Karen!" I felt elated and somewhat horrified at the same time.

Because I am married, I have not been without human contact all this time, like many. But I ached to connect physically with my friends, which is why spread-out hangs-in-yards and masked hikes in the woods were still far better than screens (at least I knew my beloved ones still had legs). But nothing, nothing compares to being able to hold another person I adore.

Since that Sunday at the lake, I have hugged exactly two other friends—only ones that I love as much as Karen—also masked and even more conscientiously—and each time has felt sinfully delicious. I can't wait to do it again.

KAREN and I are 40-something women who text day and night as needed, as wanted. For months, among sharing fun photos and interesting articles, she had texted me about her work woes as a speech-language pathologist in a demanding school environment and her complicated relationship with her mom, who had recently moved to the same town.

One morning, Karen texted me that, on top of her daily stresses at the job, the police had just called her workplace to tell her that her mom had suffered a heart attack, and they asked her to meet them at the hospital.

On my way. She texted me. *I have no idea what happened.*

Oh my God, I texted back. *Please let me know what I can do, if anything.*

I will. Just trying to drive safely right now.

(*Heart emoji*)

In retrospect, it's obvious that this tactic by the authorities is intended to ensure the person shows up. Give little detail, and make the scene urgent and vaguely mysterious, but not too scary.

Forty-five minutes passed. I went into a project meeting with my boss, and Karen sent a few more texts, which I eyed while trying to pay attention to work priorities:

They're making me wait in the 'consult room.' Alone.

Jason isn't up yet. (Her husband.)

Fuck. Why isn't anyone talking to me?

And finally, *She died, Anne.*

"I have to go," I told my boss in the middle of our conversation.

On my way.

Half an hour later, at the same window of the same local hospital where I had checked in my husband after he fell down the stairs of our first apartment and dislocated two of his fingers, where I asked the desk nurse how our friend Kevin was after collapsing on stage playing the drums, where I had been picked up after my own car crash—the same sickly yellow-lit window with the sliding Plexiglass panes, and why did that waiting room have to be so ugly?—I blurted, "Hello my friend's mom was just brought here not that long ago maybe an hour or two and I'm her friend and it was a heart attack and I'm sorry I don't remember her mom's name which is terrible but my friend's name is Karen and we don't really know what happened but I need to see her right away and she knows I'm coming and..."

And angel in scrubs asked, "Are you Anne?"

At my hurried nod, the nurse clicked the automatic double doors, which opened like wings inviting me into the ER, and she, in her white crocs, padded softly across the linoleum tiles, leading me briskly but kindly, scrub pants swishing down the hallway, slid open a door, and brushed back a curtain.

My sweet, petite friend was crouched in the single chair in the room, overlooking a hospital bed on which lay her mother's newly dead body. I did the only thing I knew to do: I threw my arms around her. As if to try to keep her intact during a moment of possible, probable, inevitable collapse, I provided a modicum of scaffolding, something to lean on, at least for a moment.

It was one of those things you never plan on and a foreign kind of emergency. Too late for anything to save her mom, I had to do what I could for my friend. Helpfully, my focus, often scattered among disparate priorities, was laser-focused. Everything in the outside world slipped away; the only thing that existed anymore was me kneeling on the floor and Karen hunched in the chair and her mom's too-still figure draped in a white sheet, her face just peering over the edge, in a shrouded, windowless white room in which we had no idea what to do next, and I had no idea what to say.

But I had one powerful tool at my disposal, and I employed it, again and again, as the reality sunk in, as the practical matters began to swirl, as the nurses intruded and asked all kinds of impossible questions, as I said goodbye when Jason showed up— and in the weeks and months ahead. I just hugged her, and hugged her, and hugged her some more. Without my arms, I would have felt entirely incompetent, but somehow, this physical gesture, this human, living touch, made a difference.

In this new season of disconnection and loss, I ache more than ever to hold the ones I love, to hold things together.

LESSONS FROM A PANDEMIC PUPPY

KIMBERLY HENSLE LOWRANCE

I've never been a dog person.

The smells, nipping, barking, drooling—none of that was for me.

Yet in early April 2020, after only a few weeks of self-quar antining with my family, I found myself perusing Petfinder the way others under a stay-at-home order made sourdough starters or refreshed their Twitter feeds. It became my new obsession.

I stood at the kitchen counter, the newspaper's obituary section too thick under my hands, the newsprint leaving shadows on my fingers, and I hoped for some way to steady myself amid all the loss and uncertainty. That's when I imag ined a fluffy Goldendoodle or faithful Labrador at my feet.

Midway through a COVID-19 news conference, the rising rates of infection making my heart race, I turned to the online profiles of available rescue dogs, falling in love with one after another. Every time remote learning and the isolation from their friends left my children in tears, I wondered if a dog might shift our mindset—from worrying to caring, from fear to solace. I started a campaign to convince my husband that it was time to adopt a dog. My first step was to email him photos of dogs. As he sat on conference calls in his temporary office in our basement, his inbox beeped with one heartwarming picture after another: puppies, young adults, seniors, all needing homes.

I never made it to step two. The photos convinced him—that and our daughter's new habit of walking around the house reading from a children's book about dogs. She cornered me in the kitchen one day, nearly yelling: "Have you ever seen a corgi? Or a French bulldog?" She waved the book in her hand. "The Cavalier King Charles spaniel makes an excellent family dog. And look how cute it is!"

She and her older brother followed up with a typed missive outlining why we should get a dog. *We promise to walk it every day*, they wrote. A first draft, handwritten by my daughter, included pencil-drawn hearts along the edge of the paper.

Their efforts to convince us to get a dog distracted them from the elimination of their childhood activities. One by one, the part of their daily lives that provided structure and fun—from school to birthday parties, from softball games to fencing tournaments—were cancelled. A dog became a symbol of what could still be possible.

Unbeknownst to my kids, by then we'd already applied to several rescue organizations. One, in Connecticut, approved us but then halted out-of-state adoptions until the pandemic receded. When I focused on Massachusetts-based rescues, I discovered I wasn't the only one interested in adoption. A shelter north of Boston indicated they'd received more than 2,000 applications to adopt or foster in the preceding month. I read about another shelter in Florida that, during the early weeks of quarantine, had adopted out all of its available pets—the first time in its history.

Happy for the animals, but discouraged for my family, I did what any self-respecting Gen Xer does while at home during a pandemic: I posted to Facebook about how hard it was to adopt a rescue dog. Within minutes, a friend introduced me to a nonprofit that saves cunucu dogs, strays from Aruba. They had one last puppy being fostered in Massachusetts. Were we interested? Yes, we absolutely were. Three days later, we brought that puppy home.

We named our new family member Zara, which means "blooming flower." We poured our hope into that name selection. We saw it as a promise that, one day, a vaccine would be found, borders would open up again, and we'd be able to leave our homes without worrying about getting sick.

We were instantly smitten with Zara, and she quickly figured us out. It took only a short while for her to understand that my daughter would carry her anywhere and that my son's lap was always available, even when he was completing his math homework (or *especially* when he was completing his math homework). She learned that I almost always had treats in my pocket, that when I opened the dishwasher there was a good chance I'd let her lick the bowls, and that my husband could regularly be counted on to play catch.

In those first few months with Zara, the shared responsibility of caring for our new addition narrowed my family's purpose down to the most essential: food, shelter, love. We all had a hand in training her and making her feel at home. Thanks to Zara's need to be walked several times a day, we regularly got outside. Most mornings, as the sun rose, I stood in my pajamas in our front yard, listening to the birds chirp and watching Zara sniff our blooming peonies. My daughter took the late morning shift, strolling with Zara in between school assignments. My son walked her around our neighborhood in the afternoon, and my husband committed to walking her before bed, as stars filled the night sky.

Zara connected us to other people, too, a marvel in the time of social distancing. Friends texted and called with training tips, my daughter introduced Zara to her buddies via Zoom, and neighbors we'd never spoken to said hello as they saw us walking by, Zara trotting at our feet.

As it became clear that quarantine life would be longer than anyone expected, our need to be in nature deepened. Zara joined us on long hikes through fields and mud and along well-worn paths. We discovered that she loved the snow and was happiest chasing after us as we snowshoed amid the New England pine trees. She even tried swimming, though she wasn't a fan. No matter the weather—sun, rain, or snow—we went outside for her, and each time we did, we breathed a little easier and found ourselves appreciating our environment in ways we hadn't before.

As the weeks passed, news reports about COVID-19 shared space with broadcasts of Black Lives Matter protesters demanding change for hundreds of years of systemic racism. Zara accompanied my family to a vigil for George Floyd, and she was at our side as we had deep conversations about race, injustice, and how we could be better allies. She sat at my feet as I camped out in front of the television, awaiting the outcome of the presidential election, and then celebrated with my family when the news came that we'd elected our first woman—and the first person of color—as vice president. When the Capitol's security was breached and our democracy was threatened on January 6, we were glued to the news coverage, and as if sensing she needed him, Zara climbed onto the couch next to my husband, pushing her nose under his arm to snuggle close. Zara was with us through all of the events of our quarantined year.

One recent morning, as the snow finally melted and the daffodils in my yard began to burst through the ground, signifying our second pandemic spring, my children slept in, my husband made us coffee, and I sat with Zara on the floor, running my fingers through her caramel-colored hair. It was one of those mornings when life felt almost normal, as if a pre-pandemic day had miraculously appeared in the middle of 2021. But I felt overwhelmed—that combination of fatigue and worry that plagued so many of us every day of the pandemic. Zara understood. She leaned against me, and our breathing moved in sync. All the questions that raced through my mind each day—Would our democracy survive? How would we heal from generations of racism? Would my children ever be able to safely return to school? How many more people would die from this pandemic? Why wouldn't people wear masks?—momentarily faded. I let go of my panic. *Slow down*, my dog seemed to say to me. *Appreciate the small moments that make up each day*.

I'm trying to hold onto her advice as we slowly move out of quarantine life. Zara will remind me, I know. Every day when I take her for a walk, she'll tug at her leash to get around the corner, to run, to find something new to sniff, to say hello to the other dogs in our neighborhood, to be in the world, to pay attention to what's in front of her. On this one thing, I'll follow her lead.

Zara's been with us for a year now. During that time, she's managed to fulfill almost every one of my concerns about getting a dog. She pooped in our living room, ate our budding hydrangea plant, ripped a hole in my slippers, destroyed a computer cord, and gnawed at the coffee table. She has grown significantly bigger than we thought she'd be, regularly sheds all over the sofa, and barks at every delivery person who comes to the front door.

I've easily forgiven her for all of her indiscretions, surprising everyone around me, myself most of all. "You're a dog person now, Mom," my daughter said by way of explanation.

She might be right.

SUBTLE SHIFTS

NATALIE SERIANNI

May 2020, 7:02 a.m.

I stumble into the kitchen and look out the window, the Seattle sun shimmering on my front lawn. I start my coffee ritual, scooping the grounds, pouring the water. It's quiet. Six weeks into our statewide lockdown, it became full-blown spring. I've noticed this; we all have. Mother Nature demanded we pay attention.

In the early days of containment, our collective minds have been working overtime: How safe is the grocery store? How do I homeschool? And even: *What are we going to do?* There is a sense of unease and swirling paranoia about what comes next.

It's eerily empty in our neighborhood: no cars, no airplanes decelerating overhead. I'm catapulted back to another quiet time in my life when I didn't drive. Where I rode bikes in the street (like my kids are now). When I was at the mercy of what was in my immediate orbit.

When the carousel grinds to a halt, and our pandemic present is too much, my mind moves to the past, right to the 1980s, where I find answers to a 20-year search for the feeling of home, and how to become whole out of pieces.

OUR 80S HOME was our touchstone. Our hearth became a stage for Pointer Sister dance parties. There were giant chocolate chip cookie cakes for birthday parties, Glade candles in the bathroom, and the smell of country store potpourri in the kitchen. It was a time of pillow forts and freeze tag in the backyard. My younger sister and I played "apartments" in our bedrooms, pretending we lived alone in New York City penthouses. I can still hear the white roller skates clinking their pink wheels down the sidewalk of our suburban Maryland home. The wind tickling my cheek as I sat and read under the weeping willow in our front yard.

There was calm and comfort in my childhood.

My Milli Vanilli and INXS posters kept watch over my *Sassy* and *Seventeen* magazines, my blue canopy bed hiding the lock & key rainbow diaries underneath. "Everybody Wants to Rule the World" and Def Leppard blasted from my bedroom speakers, making way for the ("*disturbing,*" as my mom would say, pursing her lips) Depeche Mode/Cure era that was to take hold of my teenage years.

Life was carefree with my parents and two younger sisters at home, the main character of my memories.

JUNE 2020.

At seven years old, my oldest daughter has picked up her preschool habit of collecting insects again. Bumblebees are caught. Even pill bugs and ladybugs are hunted. My three-and-a-half-year-old daughter has also joined the mix, running from one side of the backyard to the other, yelling "GOTCHA!!" while pouncing on insects with the bug catcher.

We have amassed quite a menagerie: caterpillars hibernating in their cocoons on my daughter's white dresser, awaiting their entrance into our world, and an ant farm gently shipped via FedEx, arriving on our doorstep from Burlington, North Carolina. We dumped the sand, unboxed the ants, and watched in awe as they burrowed and built their tunnels, going about their home making.

After clearing the breakfast dishes one morning, I marvel at their handiwork as they circle around: without compartments, all the routes eventually lead to the other ants. They find each other, land on each other, work with each other. All day, while the ground continually shifts beneath them.

Like the ants, I feel crowded. There is too much together time. There are piles of books, juice boxes, and crayons scattered on what was our dining room table, now our central hub. I'm not used to all of us here in the house. I like my space. My quiet office on campus is miles—and what feels like lightyears—away. Also: when did we become ok with everyone peeing with the door open?

There are days when nobody gets along, and I snap, the walls inching closer. I convince myself that I'm not failing at my teaching job while homeschooling my seven-year-old, and that *Sesame Street* is just fine for my four-year-old to watch because there is *learning*. I drink cold coffee. There is three-day-old laundry in the dryer, and I'm too tired to fold it. We're Zooming in a slog of unknowing, a heaviness of uncertainty.

In my mind, I find myself going back to the certainty of the 80s, where I roamed the neighborhood on my pink Huffy Sweet Thunder and peddled to the pool. Where my mom sang "The Sun Will Come Out Tomorrow," as she tucked us in, crocheted blankets up to our chins. We caught lightning bugs in coffee cans, and we ran through the farmer's field just before it became a new housing development.

The air carried freedom.

MARCH 2021, still COVID-times.

I feel a sting of nostalgia thinking back to my childhood when we seemed to have it all. I even had my mother, who would die from a brain aneurysm when I turned 25.

She stayed home with us, raising three daughters in a cul-de-sac Colonial home. Tree canopies and open space. We had a newly constructed back deck and a Spacemaker kitchen TV. She must have had a motherhood moment, where she proudly surveyed her domain, took a drag off her cigarette and thought: "This is it."

It jolts me back to now. *Is this the pinnacle of our parenting? In a pandemic?* Maybe this is our peak, when things feel familiar and disorienting in the same breath.

I've had this feeling before.

My traumatic entrance into motherhood in 2013 came with a seven-pound baby girl, two blood transfusions, and anxiety that stuck for one full year. When I arrived home with my oldest, on a gray, frozen January day, I walked past the hallway mirror, terrified. I did not see myself from before. I was shocked into something new.

SOMEDAYS, I feel strangely equipped during this pandemic. Having a newborn prepared me, as did years-long loneliness before becoming a mother. Loneliness had been my roommate for years, moving in right after my mother died, occupying every empty space.

Those first few weeks after my mother died in September 2001, much like during this pandemic, there was little sleep.

Nighttime is when the shifting takes place, when the cells transform. Matter searching for meaning.

After she died, my constitution couldn't go back to before. It was unthinkable. In desperation, I quit my first visiting professorship, my first job after graduate school, and moved back to my childhood home in Maryland.

I couldn't face going back to the classroom, what once was. I drove down to North Carolina, to my brand new, not even furnished apartment to pack up. With my books and a crying cat, I headed north: five dazed hours, listening to Travis and David Gray, not even in my body, the four white lanes on I-95 blinking, blurry with my tears.

I lived at home with my father for six months, watching pieces of my mother leave the house in boxes: clothes, mostly. Perfume. Her address book, bulging with notes on scraps of paper. I substitute taught at high school, answering robocalls at 5:30 a.m., saying yes to work. Saying yes to leaving the house, yes to interacting with others in their still-moving life while mine was at a standstill. I'd leave the sleepy house with my coffee, hoping to glimpse her in the kitchen. Each morning, a gut punch that she was gone. Much of me evacuated when she left; home lost its hold.

Since then, life has been a movie reel. I moved back to North Carolina and met my husband in 2005. When our eyes first locked, in the kitchen of a house party while I was standing next to my ex-boyfriend, atoms crashed. I felt the familiar spark of comfort.

We fused quickly. We yearned for bigger spaces, newness. Wildness. We searched the U.S. map and placed our fingers in the Pacific Northwest. We got as far away from North Carolina as we could go, driving cross-country, through the midline of America, past the Dakotas, and straight into marriage and a townhouse in Seattle.

My cells began to settle after we bought our first house. After getting the keys, my husband at work, I stood with my second trimester belly, looking at a Linden tree from the upstairs bedroom, feeling a century of families under my bare feet. The 1928 hardwood floors were coated with a still alive love. I allowed this house to hold me. But loneliness resided, too.

NEEDING to be alone became part of my DNA. During the hardest experiences in my life—mourning my mother, running a marathon, birthing two babies—I was, essentially, alone. Although I had the support of others, in the wings or right next to me, I still managed to push people away. I refused to be seen in my suffering or sadness—hot, heavy Mother's Day tears or throat lumps when talking with my dad. Hiding my "prickly parts" during these difficult moments, I mutated, separating from others.

For the last eight years, as a working mother of two in midlife, I've been running from work, to daycare, to preschool, to after-school soccer, to volunteering, to Girl Scouts, in a tunnel of *go*. I was a sleep-deprived, coffee-fueled shell of myself. Careening off the rails, I've been filled with fear for most of my children's life. But I pushed through because I was productive. I could handle it by myself. I didn't need help; I could *hustle*. I morphed into a lesser creature.

Driving past scenic Lake Washington on my way to work

each pre-pandemic morning, there were countless times I looked over to the passenger side, longing to dive into the freezing water— to submerge, to swim free and sure again. To startle myself awake and coalesce in the healing water.

That feeling unraveled, slowly, after several unhurried months at home with my family during this pandemic. I woke up my youngest daughter by crawling into her bed, the warm sheets, curls on her pillow, the faint smell of pee in a pull-up. We all shared breakfast and lingered over lunch. I watched my oldest daughter learn to cross the street, her long ponytail swinging as she looked both ways, me waving from the dining room window. These moments have assembled me into someone who can get close to what she loves.

My children saw their mother grinning on a stand-up paddleboard one summer moment, and rage-filled about dirty dishes the next. They saw my range; they saw me. Being home has helped me understand my own basic needs: I need my family, and they need to know who I am. I'm a mother learning to mother myself while I mother my children.

———

THE PANDEMIC WON'T ALLOW me to pretend that my hair's not gray, or that working from home with others on top of you isn't hard. From the anguish of losing my mother to the blur of the baby years, I've finally had a moment to step back and clearly see my last 20 years in full view. And just like this pandemic, they've been a marvel, and a doozy.

Often during this time of at-homeness, I've thought of the magical, beloved book I had on my own dark brown childhood bookshelf, *The Little Prince*. I remember the otherworldly, cartoonish illustrations, a boy poised on a planet. A fox. Many times during this stay-at-home mandate, and I believe now more than ever, its premise is true: "What is essential is invisible to the eye."

It's become our sole survival question this past year: *Do we have what we need?*

After a year of this pandemic, I can say: *I do now.* It's what I knew as an eight-year-old in the 80s: home is love in close proximity.

This pandemic has brought crisis and fear for many of us, but hope flitters on the horizon. Like my daughter's caterpillars who became butterflies and took off into the air, they teach us what to do: in different shapes and forms, we continue.

AT THE MOVIES

CAROLINE GRANT

When I notice Zoom sucking the life out of me, I step outside and watch a movie.

A fluke of urban planning offers my third-floor balcony a view into seven different San Francisco backyards and driveways. I used to glance out and notice how much isn't beautiful: a couple of big apartment buildings dominate the view, one shingled in pale toothpaste green, the other dirty beige. I see many rickety gutters and downspouts, grey satellite dishes, and mysterious cords whipping in the wind or snaking down the sides of buildings.

But now instead of looking out, I look down, into the yards and driveways where a different near-silent film plays wherever I look. The movies unspooling in my neighbors' outdoor spaces offer a nice break from the repetitive story being written in my own house. I'm Jimmy Stewart in *Rear Window*, without the camera or the fevered imagination.

Next door, the yard is bursting with dahlias and roses; lemon and plum trees hang heavy with fruit. Three generations live in this house, but the grandmother is the only one I ever see in the yard, walking a tight rectangle around her flower beds, pausing occasionally for her tai chi.

The adjacent backyard is as bare as its neighbor is blooming. It's entirely paved, with a storage shed hulking in the back and rows of plastic boxes and milk crates lining the fences, but a pigtailed child runs tight circles on the concrete while her mom and grandma chat across the fence with their neighbor, speaking a language I don't know. When I hear her sneakers smacking the pavement, I step away from my desk and go stretch on my balcony, as if I could soak up some of her energy.

In the other direction, a twenty-something woman, her hair in a ballerina bun, glides back and forth on roller blades, swaying to the music piping in from her earbuds. A towering redwood shades her driveway, pulling my focus away from the parked car and the garbage bins. It's so quiet and still—with just a light wind stirring the branches and the barest scrape of her blades on the sidewalk—she could be a skater on a frozen New England pond.

Two houses away, a stage is set over the course of a few days. First, two kettle grills are rolled onto the concrete patio; then a string of lights goes up; then some delicate white paper pennants, like a length of doilies, are hung across the yard. They flutter brightly in the breeze.

I'm wondering whether it will be a graduation party or a birthday, when late one afternoon a small group gathers: bride, groom, parents, and two attendants in matching purple. The fog billows down from Sutro Tower but the women seem immune to the cold in their sleeveless dresses. I watch them from my balcony, texting with friends, "A wedding! So sweet!" One asks if the guests are masked or keeping distant, and although the virus is stressing me out and I haven't been more than four miles from my home in three months, I text back, "No! Don't care. Wedding!!" The party lingers outside past dark, exchanging toasts, dancing to music on a phone. I can still hear it, a little tinny and distant, punctuated by short bursts of laughter, when I go to bed that night.

We're all living so much on our screens these days that these glimpses of other lives are as transporting as any glossy travel show. I take a break from my writing to imagine little stories about them as I stretch my legs on the balcony. These neighbors —strangers to me, living differently under the same constraints as I—offer a sweet escape into other worlds.

My family watches actual movies to escape, too. I choose Ken Burns' documentary about the national parks system to make up for a cancelled spring break trip to Yosemite. My dad, who moved out of his assisted living community to shelter with us, chooses to revisit a slew of Alec Guinness comedies from the '40s and '50s, most of which haven't aged as well as my dad. My 15-year-old history buff chooses *The Darkest Hour*, *The Bridge on the River Kwai*, and *They Shall Not Grow Old*. We all choose to leave realism behind with *Shaun of the Dead*, *The Invisible Man*, *Blade Runner*, and *2001: A Space Odyssey*. They're dark, but they're not COVID-dark. For a couple of hours a night, we crowd around the television and enter a world untouched by this disease.

Escaping feels okay, feels self-protective and even wise, until George Floyd's murder shakes me right out of that mindset.

SO I START to push our movie choices in a different direction. We watch an Agnès Varda documentary on the Black Panthers and another about James Baldwin visiting groups of Black teenagers in 1960s San Francisco—both heartbreaking because of how little has changed. We lift our spirits with a documentary about Oakland elementary schoolers participating in a speech festival named for Martin Luther King, Jr., and another one about Congressman John Lewis. We watch films by Spike Lee, Julie Dash, and Ava DuVernay.

We're not escaping but looking at things from a different perspective, looking at things more critically. It's a small first step toward reentering—and working to change—our difficult world.

Because the world is starting to reopen and how do we want to find it? I'm organizing voters, writing to my representatives, signing petitions, making donations. There's plenty to do from inside.

And I shift my focus at the window, too. I don't know these neighbors and I still keep to myself on the balcony, but now when I see them, I don't make up stories for myself anymore. It's no longer my escape but their futures I imagine: the grandma, the pigtailed child, the rollerblader, the newly-married couple— I'm planning for better days. For all of us.

THE BIG CHOP

CHANIZE THORPE

Cutting my long locs in the wake of COVID-19 led to a discovery of a new grade of hair and a fear my short style wouldn't be accepted in the dating world.

For two decades I had permanent dreadlocs—a style that can usually only be removed by cutting off the majority of one's hair. Seeking a change and knowing I couldn't maintain my locs during the COVID-19 pandemic, I lopped it all off. The result was both elation and terror looking at my new 'do. *Omg, what have I done?* was the big question. That was followed by the harrowing thought that I'd be considered unattractive to people who like long hair.

As a 48-year-old African-American woman, I've had a life-long struggle with my hair. When I was a young girl, I had to endure hot-combing to "tame" my thick head bush. It was a process that was popular for little Black girls back in the day—one that many grew to hate. The sizzling comb was heated on the stove and applied to our "nappy" hair, as we suffered through sitting very still, the smell of scorching hair, and nervousness when the hot comb came close to your ear or forehead. (I don't know anyone who hasn't been burned by a hot comb.) The idea was to straighten it out, based on the belief that straight hair made you look more "presentable" to the world.

Relaxers in my teens were a nightmare of chemicals designed to break down what seemed like a bird's nest. I used to go to a salon called Black Hair Is, in Harlem—on a Saturday, you'd see dozens of women getting the "creamy crack" applied to their scalp. At 25, I chose to grow dreadlocs, a natural style requiring minimal maintenance, as I was tired of the effort required by relaxers. It felt like I was in the salon every two weeks. I decided that Mother Nature obviously wanted me to do something different: go natural. It seemed I had finally found the perfect style for me.

However, 22 years later, after traumatic events, including a bitter divorce, I ached for a change. I believed my hair was holding in decades of bad energy, so I decided to make the Big Chop. I cut my shoulder-length hair off with only an inch of virgin hair left and had it styled into a little afro. I wanted to start again and build healthier roots for my scalp and more importantly, my *soul*.

I found my stylist, Andre Tinnie, a natural hair expert based in Brooklyn, NY, about ten years earlier when my previous stylist had started doing more weaves and didn't have time to see me. Several people in my Facebook dreadloc group had recommended him. Andre has performed his fair share of life-altering cuts. "My clients normally feel a sense of relief, liberation, and that a burden has been lifted off their shoulders," he says. Some had different reactions. "They had total regret at first, then after a few weeks they embraced the change." In true fashion, when sitting in a hairdresser's chair, a form of therapy happens.

I went to the salon. Andre knew what I was going to do, so he made sure I was his only client for a number of hours. He sat me in the chair and asked me if I was sure I wanted to do this. I looked in the mirror for a minute, took a deep breath, and said yes. He turned the chair away from the mirror and started cutting. My stylist didn't let the hair fall to the floor, though, and put the locs in a bag. After he finished cutting, he took me to the sink and applied dye to my hair. I still didn't know what I looked like. I think he didn't want me to see until he finished.

When he turned the chair to the mirror, I gasped and some tears fell, but it looked better than I thought it would. I gave him a big hug when I left. I couldn't stop looking at myself in store windows; on the subway, I wondered if people could tell what I had just done. I kept looking at the bag of hair and couldn't believe how long it was. When I got home, my friend shrieked that she loved it. I shed a few more tears, but I was smiling too.

I'm still trying to adjust to my new short hair and a curl pattern I never knew I had (4c); I didn't love it at first, because it was such a dramatic change. After having had hair past my shoulders, it's quite an adjustment to now have a small afro. Managing without my stylist during the pandemic has been difficult to say the least. I don't feel comfortable making the two-hour trek to see him, which would require me to either drive and struggle to find parking in New York City, or take mass transportation several times, wear a mask, and fight off the panic of being in an enclosed space. Right now I feel vanity isn't that important. Besides, it's not like I'm going anywhere special any time soon.

So I'm maintaining my pandemic haircut by myself and belong to a hair styling group to get advice and ideas on different techniques that were foreign to me before I made the chop. It's refreshing to see so many Black women showing how beautiful short and natural hair can be. I feel there's also more acceptance in the media, more people who have embraced natural hair and look amazing.

But I wasn't expecting the amount of criticism I received from family and people I dated. They lamented my lack of long locs with surprised comments of "Why did you do that?" It made me feel like my hair was something people associated me with, and I didn't like that. The most hurtful comment from a male family member was: "You look like a man."

After I made the chop, I posted a picture on social media and said, "New year, new 'do." Most of the responses were positive. There were a few "Omg" comments, and "Where'd your hair go?" was a common question. The "Why?" remarks came mostly from men, and I said that I wanted a new start but didn't get defensive. I believe a lot of men feel women should have long hair; it's almost as if they fetishize it. When family members criticized me, it stung a little, but I didn't give them the satisfaction of getting angry and instead just changed the subject. Ultimately, I didn't regret my choice.

My stylist has had plenty of discussions with women who were afraid their partner wouldn't be attractive to them anymore after cutting off their coiffure. I can relate to that feeling. Even though we were divorced, my ex-husband felt the need to share his thoughts on my change—though I never asked him for his opinion. I had straight hair when we met. When I'd told him what I was going to do, he wasn't pleased. His comments made me wonder if I'd find another partner who would accept me as I am. I was self-conscious when looking for a potential romantic partner in the dating scene; my anxiety worsened when folx would check out my social media pics and videos.

I've realized several things during this pandemic. I'm not alone in feeling the need to reinvent myself, no matter if it's a haircut, job, or relationship. The decision to make the "Big Chop" is highly personal, and the more support one has, the easier the transition. My best friends, my new partner—who has short hair, like me—and my online hairstyle community have been instrumental in praising my hair and reaffirming that I made the right decision. I now know I'm not alone in feeling conflicted about my choices, and I'm still excited for things to come. It's getting easier for me to understand it's *just hair*. Hopefully, I'll get to know more about the person most important on this journey—me. I'm getting there, one style at a time.

ESSENTIAL

MARYA ZILBERBERG

My kids have become nocturnal. Like the mice that live in the walls of my old farmhouse, they turn industrious after darkness falls. Maybe it's their age. More likely it's their schedules fractured by the pandemic, a predictable rhythm of college life interrupted by this viral intruder that refuses to respect boundaries, making light superfluous. My son and daughter are both here, in our pandemic pod, stuck—extraverted youth derailed into forced insularity with their rapidly aging mothers.

From my bed in the thick darkness, I hear their footsteps— my six-foot son's paradoxically quiet, like padded feet of a cat; my daughter's like an infantry man's. They have always been like this, even *in utero*. His ultrasound peek found him floating in the amniotic fluid with the equanimity of the Buddha, sucking his fingers, the same ones he would suck to soothe himself after he popped out. When my spouse was pregnant with our daughter, we used to lie in bed and watch her globular belly, its skin shiny and taut, peak like a tidal wave, as our fetal girl put herself through her paces, elbows and heels cresting and falling. Sometimes we'd grab her by what felt like a foot, and she would yank it with surprising deftness and whoosh it over to the opposite side away from our grasp. As a child, she would toddle over to our bed and insert herself diagonally between us, thrashing in her sleep, pushing us to the very edges.

My kids' small, predictable actions are comforting amidst raging uncertainty. Some nights the aromas of broth and sesame oil waft up as they cook Ramen. Its residue lingers into the morning hours, smelling like a distant skunk in light distress. Peals of laughter awaken me at three a.m. as she shows him some funny character she's created on her iPad, or as they commune virtually with their pals, similarly imprisoned in their families' homes.

Like the careening mice whose ghostly presence I see in tiny piles of plaster dust in the corners, the kids leave traces for me in the morning: a few grains of rice on the granite counter, a pan on the stove with a single dried noodle stuck to its side. It annoys me when they don't clean up after themselves, but it's an insignificant annoyance, and I cherish my quiet mornings in a tidy kitchen too much to wake them up. So I pick up while the kettle boils.

MY BODY HAS BEEN BREAKING down in petty and ill-timed ways. I postponed my eye surgery when the winter and willful denial from the president and his henchmen accelerated the infections. Early in the quarantine, I watched a crown from one of my teeth tumble into the sink and disappear down the drain, as I frantically tried to halt its slide. I froze, stupefied, fearing having to deal with it, having to actually call the dentist, fearing the hour in his chair with my jaws prised open, the whining drill spraying chips of my tooth onto the dam stretched like a trampoline across my mouth. I stood there plotting the dismantling of the trap, the fishing out of the crown from a tangle of hair and soap I would invariably find there. My rational spouse prevailed, and I decided to let it go, convinced in the end that there would be no way to get it clean enough to be of any use, even as a temporary mitigation.

The pandemic gave me an excuse to delay seeing the dentist until after I am vaccinated. Instead, I ordered a fix-it-yourself temporary tooth kit. It's still sitting on my desk, but in researching it, I learned of a whole underworld devoted to the amateur art of home-based dentistry, spawned of pecuniary necessity by those who serve us in our time of need, and whom we forsake in theirs.

The house and its appliances have taken a hit. My main oven's heating element decided it had had enough, and went on a strike last March, just as I slid my first sourdough loaf in. Before closing the door and walking away, my brain caught up with my senses, and I realized the oven was only lukewarm. I've limped through the pandemic using my much smaller side oven, determined to continue with my inchoate homesteading.

The plumbing has suffered too, no longer willing to put up with such steady use. First, it was the shower in the master bathroom—the leak underneath prompted a ceiling demolition. Freed pieces of plaster and a steady stream of water trickled down a funnel we created from a green plastic tablecloth and tacked up to point the fallout into a bucket while we waited for our plumber to show up, masked and heavy-booted, and shut off the water. The kids' bathroom went next when we discovered a drip-drip downstairs below it. The plumber had to return, tramping in the unseasonable mud. We are now down to a single shower and only two toilets that work. This is still more than what I had during my childhood in a communal flat in Odessa, Ukraine, where five families shared a single toilet, where we had no hot water, and where on Sundays we trudged a mile to a public bathhouse for our weekly shower. I worry that, before this pandemic is over, we'll return to boiling water and a make-shift tub in the kitchen, the way my parents bathed me when I was small.

It's not just dental work or ovens or plumbing. We have all learned to live without things we had once considered indispensable: haircuts, dinners out, parties with friends, book readings, theater, live music and dance, and fondling produce at the market. Last December we had our holidays via Zoom, along with most of the world in this aberration of a year, and raised our distant glasses to better times to come. We've thanked those we call "essential," and while we are sincere in our gratitude, in the secret corners of our souls we are also grateful not to be one of them. Because in this country at this time, "essential" rhymes with "disposable."

I am lucky that my home office continues to function as it did in the more normal times. I haven't traveled in over a year, and I cannot say I miss it: everything I need is already here.

Yet none of it had to be this way; not all the death, nor the threat of becoming severely ill, nor the duration of our isolation. All it would have taken was some effort, some humble deference to experts, some give-and-take from the citizenry, some minute amount of discipline in exchange for the privilege of a semi-normal life, some minuscule realization that we were all requisite to the effort. Instead, the lies gushed like in my old country, and many believed. So they refused, all of it. Every refusal had its own calculus, its own perverse priority, a nihilistic drive to destroy. None of it was surprising in a society where the Second Amendment is stifling the First, where guns have more rights than people, where freedom is a one-way street, and where the doublespeak of "All Lives Matter" is a confession of its dark opposite.

My privilege has come into full focus. It has taken the pandemic for me to grok the magnitude of our national disrepair, so quotidian to the lives of so many whom we call essential. My own local disintegrations pale in comparison, and maybe this explains the sanguine attitude I've taken toward all the breaking and disuse in my person and my home, which in a normal year would have seemed galling and somehow unjust. This year I just turn toward what is not broken.

These days, weeks, months will forever be just another incongruity of frustration and fury and shock, and also this unforeseeable bonus of having my fledglings at my side for just a little longer, confined to my nest not by some despotic will of my own, but by a hurricane of circumstances beyond our control.

As vaccination programs begin to put an end to this quarantine, our worlds will re-expand into some semblance of their pre-pandemic size. Will our more persistent plagues—complacency, tribalism, racism, xenophobia—continue to devour us? Will our culture continue to decay, seduced by false dichotomies that win elections, but dig us deeper into rubble? The choice is ours, at least at this moment. Perhaps surviving this year of captivity, on top of the previous three which have illuminated our festering historical wounds, will not have been in vain. They say sunshine is the best disinfectant. I hope so.

A FEW WEEKS AGO, another one of my crowns failed. The right side of my mouth is doing all the hard work for now. But as afraid as I am of dentists, it won't be long until I am out of excuses for not getting it fixed. I am gearing up for my eye surgery too. The oven and the plumbing will come next.

The kids are less ambivalent about our impending liberation from this prolonged and, at times, claustrophobic gestation. My son cannot wait to go to the movies with his friends, to have their help with his car restoration, to breathe the same air they breathe without the obstacles of masks and apprehension. My daughter is eager to travel, to see the corners of the world and the corners of her friends' mouths in the flesh. She is moving out to an apartment with her new pod in preparation for a limited return to campus. Their lives are about to shift back into daylight.

I will lie in my bed in the darkness listening for their footsteps, for their laughter and voices. My nose will search for the scent of their midnight snacks. In the morning, I will examine the kitchen for crumbs of their nocturnal escapades and find none. The pounding that wakes me will be rain on the roof or the wall critters going on with their business. I will imagine my daughter in her new apartment, sitting on her bed, her face lit up by her iPad screen, as she creates heads and eyes and ears and hair and torsos and appendages of characters who by the morning, through the magic of her apps, will be moving and laughing and speaking and building their bright and as yet uncharted worlds.

SOON

LAURIE FOOS

My son has always had fears. New places. New bus drivers. Getting lost in a store. He's afraid I'll disappear. When he was little, he feared the Tooth Fairy.

"Why is she little?" he asked me once in a panic, flapping his arms and jumping up and down. "Why does she go in kids' rooms?"

Back then, we compromised by leaving the tooth under the pillow in my room, not his. But when he lost a tooth this past January—even though he's almost as tall as I am now and has the beginnings of a mustache, he still has a few teeth left to lose —he agreed to leave the tooth under his own pillow, since he was sleeping in my room on a cot, where he has slept for the majority of the pandemic. During COVID, I've sometimes looked back with almost a kind of nostalgia about the fears when he was little, about how easy it was to solve the Tooth Fairy problem. Some of those fears have lingered, though, even now that he is fourteen.

My son has autism and intellectual disabilities. He is terri-fied of the virus. I am a single mom to two kids, my son Zachariah and my daughter Ella, a neurotypical teen a year older than he is. At the beginning of the pandemic, my son was still in middle school, my daughter a freshman. We've been in the house, at the time of this writing, for 392 days. (My daughter has kept count). I have not seen another adult except for doctors other than their father, from whom I've been separated since early 2017. My kids have been home, learning virtually, for the duration. Everyone else—my students, friends, colleagues—I see via Zoom.

I am fortunate to have a job that allows me to be at home, or I would have had to find some solution for the kids to remain virtual. I don't know what that solution might have been, since, as is the case with most parents of children with special needs, I cannot just hire any babysitter to take care of my son. I am a writer and teach in two low-residency creative writing programs, the residencies for which have all moved to Zoom.

Despite any number of social stories, I still have not been successful in entirely eradicating his fear of a new bus driver, a fear he has had since he was five. In his mind, a new bus driver means, *The bus driver doesn't know the way to school, and I will get lost and never get home again.* Or, at least, as best as I am able to burrow my way inside his mind and to determine from what he can articulate to me (and I am thankful every day that he has the language to articulate so much), that is what a different bus driver represents to him. Through the help of his private psychologist, I've been able to quell those fears for him. Quiet them. Mitigate them. Make them manageable.

But how do you make manageable the fears of a pandemic for a child with intellectual disabilities? Or for anyone, for that matter?

"The way to help anxiety is through exposure," his psychologist said to me via telehealth at the beginning of the pandemic, "but of course, exposure, in this case, isn't safe."

Last spring, he'd call to me every night from his cot.

"Mommy, when will the coronavirus go away?" he'd say.

I'd scramble for some kind of answer.

"I don't know, baby," I'd say. "Soon, I hope."

"I want it to go away," he said.

"Me, too," I said. "I want it to go away, too."

"Soon," he'd say. "It will go away soon. Soon it's going to disappear."

I didn't tell him that no one knew whether this was true. He'd say it to himself quietly until he fell asleep. *Soon, soon, soon.*

BACK IN MARCH, when COVID hit, online learning wasn't initially problematic. The high school determined that all learning would be moved to Google classroom with no live Google meets, and all grades would be Pass/Fail. This took the pressure off my daughter, still adjusting to high school demands. For my son, then still in middle school and in a self-contained classroom of five kids, his teacher gave the parents a blessed amount of leeway.

"There's work if you want it," she said when she called me, and I said, "I don't want it." We both laughed. She'd been his teacher for three years and knew Zachariah as well as—and in many ways, better than—I knew him myself. She set up Google meets periodically with the other kids, which he sometimes wanted to attend and sometimes didn't. She knew that my work hadn't stopped, that I still had student manuscripts to read, my own work pressures and deadlines. She knew how hard it was to balance teaching and having kids at home. She let us be.

Last spring, we did what most people were doing: we stayed at home. Everything was closed. My ex-husband, who had lost his job just prior to COVID, did all of the food shopping, drugstore runs, all of the things I didn't want to do. He stayed in the house with us most days, which became both strange and not, and which left me time to keep up with my teaching. Over Zoom calls, I talked my students down when they felt there was nothing left to write about, and no one to care about anything they'd written. *Who would care about their stories if the world was ending?* they'd lament. I gave them pep talks, reminded them that the world still turned, that people were still struggling with all of the parts of the human condition they always had. I gave them prompts. I gave them pep talks. I told them that every writer feels despair at one time or another.

I did not tell them that I was not writing. I did not tell them that the pipeline to my unconscious seemed to have sealed itself up, that my brain felt thick and heavy with pandemic fog, just as theirs did.

Aside from nights when he'd ask when the virus would disappear, though, mostly my son was calm and happy, even. He loved being at home. I'd relaxed any and all rules. Who cared in a pandemic how many video games he played? Who cared how much time he spent on his iPad?

The kids and I stayed up late, slept in, watched movies we'd seen gazillions of times. In some ways, there was even a sense of relief in those early weeks and even months. Now that every-thing was canceled, now that no one was seeing friends or family for dinners or holidays, I no longer had to explain why we might not be able to come. I no longer had to explain that our going anywhere has always been a series of internal negotiations for me, about whether traveling 45 minutes to our nearest family and friends would be worth hearing his protests about not wanting to go, or whether we'd get there and he'd beg to go home. I no longer had to worry, *Will there be too much noise? Too many people? Will I be miserable once we get there when he complains the whole time?* When I was still married, at least I had another pair of hands, another body to take him for a walk or let me have an uninterrupted conversation with one of my cousins without worrying about Zachariah, just for a little while. Having a child with special needs colors every aspect of my life. This is not a complaint, just a truth.

"You know," my daughter said, "in a lot of ways, our lives really haven't changed that much."

We both laughed. It was true. My daughter wants to be a visual artist and has always been content to be at home in her room, working on her art. As a writer, I value my alone time, when I can get any. Still, the comment stung. We had become so isolated. With my parents gone and my younger brother having decided not to speak to me for the past three years, we have almost no family left. The divorce had been isolating, and having a family member with disabilities is also often isolating. I worried about my daughter being away from her friends. I worried, as I so often do, how having a sibling with special needs impacts her. I worried about the kids getting sick, and about getting sick myself. My mother died on a respirator; I know intimately what such a death looks like. I worried about what might happen if I got sick, about who would take care of the kids, and especially about who would take care of Zachariah. I am his lifeline. I am the one who understands him best. Their father has been generous in his financial support, but his understanding of Zachariah's needs was certainly a factor in the divorce. And I worried about who would take care of me if I got sick.

As the year has gone on, that has not changed. For the most part, that is what I do: I worry, and I worry, and I worry.

MY SON also has what I call "a wonky immune system." There are things that happen with him that compromise his immunities. He is a human being and deserves privacy, and so I do not describe to anyone, really, how those issues impact his daily life. Typical high school students were offered the option to return for hybrid learning (two days in school, three days at home). My daughter did not feel safe going back. Special needs kids, because of a charge led by many parents of special needs kids, would return to school for five days. But not Zachariah. That, too, felt isolating, as I read post after Facebook post clamoring for kids to return to school. My son would remain at home, so I stayed quiet.

IN SEPTEMBER, Zachariah transitioned to high school. He lost his 1:1 aide because he would not be in the classroom. Because COVID had hit while he was still in middle school, I had never visited the program and knew little of what to expect. With two brand new teachers and no one he knew well enough to rely on, I knew his intense fears of the virus would never allow him to attend mentally. Through a series of talks with the teachers and administrators, I negotiated his online time to three periods a day. There was no possible way that he could mentally attend for six periods a day—not for him or for me.

During the first week of school, the math teacher had him doing place values. I sat at the table with him, just out of screen. I wanted the teacher to have the opportunity to form a rapport with Zachariah, and also, I did not want to start the precedent of being his 1:1 aide. I kept my own laptop out and answered emails while he worked. At first, Zachariah worked quietly, but then out of the corner of my eye, I could see him pulling at the front of his hair and heard him quoting from movies under his breath. When I looked over at the screen, I saw that the teacher had given him numbers in the millions.

My son has an IQ of 70. I swallowed my fury and told the teacher that we would need to end for the day.

"He's getting agitated," I said, and before the teacher had time to protest, I clicked the red button and hung up the call.

"School's over for the day, bud," I said in a cheery voice. "Go play Minecraft."

Zoom and Google meets are ableist systems. This is not the fault of the teachers. I explained to them as best I could what he can and cannot do. I also empathized, as a teacher myself, how difficult it must be to manage a classroom filled with students and one student online.

Slowly, things began to improve. They learned the things he likes best: Minecraft, superheroes, pizza, McDonald's. We've made s'mores pies at home in our kitchen while the kids in person worked in the kitchen that is part of the Life Skills program. He's learned to set his own alarm to wake up in the morning. He microwaves his own French fries. He got a new bed and finally moved back into his own bedroom.

AS TIME WENT on and we continued to stay at home, though, I felt a split with some of the people that I knew. Most of my friends and some family members, like us, still stayed at home. But some began to resume their lives and sometimes expected me to do the same. The parents at the high school clamored for the school to return to the full five days. I got into Facebook spats. I told people to stop gaslighting those of us for whom remote learning was not an "option." A family member shamed me with the words, "You go ahead and keep hiding in your house." My older brother argued with me about the protests in the streets and told me to "stop hiding under the bed." We have not spoken in six months. When I approached my younger brother and begged him to reconcile, told him that I feared the pain of our not speaking during a pandemic, about the terrible guilt one of us would feel if the worst happened, he refused.

―――――――

IT IS APRIL. My son's voice is changing. He now sounds like Peter Brady with the cracks and trills from their "Time to Change" music video. He has a mustache that he's learned to trim with a lady trimmer the size of a lipstick tube. My daughter has remained on the Honor Roll. One of my students had a first story published; another had an agent interested in her work. I have finally begun to write again and recently finished a middle-grade novel about siblings where one is on the autism spectrum.

We are still at home. I have had my first vaccine. We are healthy. We go to the park and wear our masks and my son rides his scooter. He is calm, and he is happy, and when he asks when the virus is going to go away, I say the thing that keeps him calm. "Soon."

SWATHED IN THICK BLANKETS: A PANDEMIC PASSAGE

TABITHA NORDBY

Wake up! It's the first week of the lockdown, and you've been thrust into a game of emotional double-dutch, tripping over the twin ropes of excitement and anxiety. Though you're forced to work from home, there's freedom in this new routine and you relish it. You can play your own music, loudly. You can choose coffee breaks as you need them. Lunch can be homemade or delivered. You can work in mismatched pajamas.

As March stumbles into April, you realize the freedom is a deception. Your Spotify playlists have become redundant, you're constantly caffeinated without the breaks, and your pants are cutting into your waistline from an abundance of UberEats deliveries. Plus, you long to wear dresses and cute shoes again.

You get up, brush your teeth, pull on a clean-ish sweater, and log on for courses with your college students. By the third week of classes, fewer of them are attending and you don't blame them; you'd rather not attend either. The stress of confinement builds in your body until one day the pressure releases into a full-blown panic attack and you are forced to cancel class in the middle of a presentation.

You log off and retreat to your bedroom. Lie down. Try to

breathe. You are convinced you are dying but don't have the energy to call 911. You wonder what your partner will do when he comes home to find your body, curled up and clenched tight, devoid of life. You get through the rest of the day swathed in thick blankets.

YOU TRY TO WAKE UP. Set your alarm for 15 more minutes. Change your mind, turn off your alarm, and sleep until noon. It's early May and you no longer have classes to teach, but a growing pile of marking awaits you on your kitchen table.

You pull yourself out of bed, leave the blankets heaped next to your sleeping cats, and trudge to the bathroom. Maybe you'll brush your teeth. Probably you won't. You stare at yourself in the mirror: frizzy hair, bleary eyes, double chin, and that one stubborn hair, now graying, wriggling out from the center of the mole on your right cheek. You make a note to avoid future confrontations with your mirror self and walk to the kitchen.

As the coffee percolates, you check your phone, hoping for something that will wake you up: an email from a friend, a high score on your latest game obsession, or new funds mysteriously added to your bank account. When the coffee's done, you add a tablespoon of cream and bring it to the living room couch. You bury yourself in a blanket fuzzy with cat hair and turn on the TV to find your next Netflix binge. Forget the marking. Don't leave this fortress except for bathroom breaks and coffee refills.

BY LATE MAY you don't even hear the alarm. The sun is hanging halfway in the sky outside your bedroom window. It is

2 p.m. You consider waking, the thought of coffee and bacon nearly luring you away from the bed. Instead, you roll over and fall back into the promising erasure of sleep. Your partner comes home at 5:00 and finds you still sleeping in a burrow of sweaty blankets. As you drag yourself out of bed, the musk of your own body wafts up from the sheets. You now smell as feral as you look, but taking a shower requires too much energy.

You order cheeseburgers and gravy-smothered fries for dinner. You and your partner watch unfunny sitcoms until it's 10 p.m. and time for him to go to bed. You dread this time of night; he gets to sleep and then leaves for work in the morning, while you are stuck here, destined to repeat this pandemic version of *Groundhog Day* over and over and over.

IT'S BECOMING difficult to wake up. Your friends and family want you to talk to a therapist, but you are reluctant because *real* devastation is striking everywhere. By June, the COVID death toll rises too rapidly for the media to keep count. Minneapolis burns with fires of rage and injustice. People lose their jobs, their homes. Victims of domestic abuse find themselves in a double bind lockdown. *You* are healthy and white, have a secure job, and live in a comfortable home in a middle-class neighbourhood with your kind and supportive (and also white) male partner.

You spend hours crying to a friend who reminds you that depression doesn't discriminate. You schedule an appointment with your therapist, and it is surprisingly effective. When the session ends you can breathe, fully and cleanly. You catch your image on the black screen of your computer and notice a faint smile on your lips. You take a hot shower and change into a fresh, matching loungewear set.

You decide to take your therapist's advice and gift yourself a creative space to play. You clean out the spare bedroom and turn it into a studio. You line the shelves with books on writing, creativity, and art. You load the cupboards with notebooks and paints and frame inspirational posters for the walls. This will be your new kingdom. You will live here in this room, being creative and productive until the world calls an all-clear and you can walk beyond your front doorstep again.

THE ALARM GOES off at 8:30, but you are already awake, and your body hums with energy. You are cozied in your egg chair in the front room, bathed in the early summer sun, and surrounded by down pillows and the deep purring of the two cats on your lap. You are writing. For 15 minutes with a group of strangers online, but you are writing! You relax into the rhythm of your pen scratching the page and you write, unencumbered, alive and attuned to this gift, this desire, this *need*.

After, you walk to the kitchen to assemble a (healthy!) breakfast of avocado toast and turkey bacon. You sit in the sun, savoring each bite slowly, promising yourself that this is the face of your new life. It is a Monday, so the new you is launched on a new week, everything perfectly aligned. You load up your favorite Spotify list, crank it, and sing along to all the songs at full voice.

IT'S 9 a.m. and the first day of your summer holidays. You can't travel or visit family, but you can luxuriate in the sun and dirt in your backyard garden. You pull weeds and imagine the harmony of purple and yellow blooms filling the space by late

July. You spend the afternoon reading in the deep-cushioned patio chair under the pergola you and your partner built. The book is cliché and a little dull but reading in the yard feels like a visit and you're undernourished in the visitation department right now.

You take a break from reading to refill your coffee and notice a voice message from work. An online meeting has been called for 2 p.m., and the dean, an HR rep, and the union rep will all be attending. Your morning Zen state disappears, replaced with a cold dread that starts in your stomach and sits lodged in your throat. You practice deep breathing for a few minutes before the meeting starts, but it does little to allay your anxiety.

You log on and are met by serious faces and strained smiles. The cold moves up your throat into your head, which is now a balloon barely tethered to your body. You attempt to maintain a smile as they inform you of the program's closure and the removal of your position and your official layoff date. The balloon is coming untethered now, and you don't register the words being spoken by the talking heads on your screen.

You text your partner and your best friend the news and then sink into the couch and numb yourself with five straight hours of the *Dynasty* reboot because trauma goes down easier with a chaser of melodrama.

YOU'VE ABANDONED YOUR ALARM; you're not falling asleep until the early morning hours anyway. Insomnia has visited you before, but this is a whole new monster. It attacks you just before midnight and pries your eyes open until daylight appears around the frame of your bedroom curtains. You fall asleep at 7 or 8 or 9 a.m. and don't wake up until most are finishing their workday.

The restrictions have loosened so you can visit with others outside. You spend July and August with friends at a neighbour's pool in a blur of water, sun, and white wine spritzers. September ushers in the return of the work and school week, and you miss the classroom and your students and the energy of teaching. By October, the days become one long endless day in which you barely exist. You feel like an extension of your couch, as dusty and worn out as the rest of your furniture.

As November brings the second lockdown, depression holds you down in its possessive grip. You try to break free of it, away from it and back into your writing, but the thought of expending creative energy exhausts you. The COVID numbers are increasing, and your insomnia is increasing, and everything seems too bleak to bother.

BY DECEMBER'S END, you are ready for change. You decide January's mantra will be "moving forward" and you embrace that by buying a planner, creating a schedule, and signing up for several writing workshops. You follow through this time. Although lockdown is still in effect, you have broken free of your internal quarantine and are ready to start over. You meditate every morning, restart a daily writing practice, and set goals for each day. Checking off a completed goal, even as minor as brushing your teeth or making your bed, feels like a small victory and propels you from one day into the next.

You start writing with a purpose. You enter a writing contest, write for deadlines, and work on finding your voice. By the end of February, you've written two pieces, you have a routine, and you begin to see your job loss as a new opportunity to pursue old dreams.

YOU WAKE up refreshed and rested by 9 a.m. The days bring more promise than despair now. Meditate. Journal. Write. Breathe. Do it all over again and keep doing it.

The pandemic is not over. You will not receive your vaccine for a while yet, but hope is revived with the coming Spring. Buds begin to appear on the trees outside your window, the air is fresh and losing its winter chill, and you've started to plan your summer garden.

You are no longer in a skip rope competition with yourself. Instead, you are taking small steps, living moment by moment, building your momentum until you are ready to walk down the path of this new journey.

STITCHING MY WAY THROUGH THE PANDEMIC

JODIE SADOWSKY

As my in-laws downsized over the years, my already cluttered home brimmed with their cast-offs: Peter Rabbit ceramic plates, a crocheted *Bless This Mess* pillow, gray knit lederhosen from my husband's childhood, and a 1912 Singer sewing machine that once belonged to my husband's great-grandmother.

The Peter Rabbit dishes were the first ones my kids grabbed from the kitchen drawer for snacks. The retro pillow sat in our playroom, reminding me just before I started to yell, that generations of children had and would act the same. They've made couch forts they'll never take apart. Spilled popcorn they'll never clean up. Removed socks they'll never put in the laundry hamper. I can't explain why I kept the lederhosen—we're not German and my five-, ten- and thirteen-year-olds have long outgrown being wrestled into them.

Set in its bulky maple cabinet, the black, red, and gold hand-painted sewing machine never matched our clean-lined West Elm furniture. We relegated it ten years ago to a mishmash corner of our basement beside our similarly neglected treadmill and wedding china. At the time, I was a real estate lawyer with a toddler and a baby on the way.

Sewing wasn't on my agenda when I took in the machine, but I must have had a hazy recall of my teenage interest in sewing. I've fact-checked this: I titled my middle-school autobiography, *A Fashion Designer, That's Me*. I loved my home economics teacher, Mrs. Whitaker, and spent as many quarters with her as I could in her sewing room and kitchen. I remember dipping peanut butter buckeyes in chocolate and sewing a stuffed rabbit with long ivory ears and a green flowered dress. My homemaker hobbies ended when I went to an intensely academic high school (though I did attempt a "quilt in a weekend" project one college winter break which, alas, I haven't yet finished).

I always said I got "mixed up with the law," my shorthand for the confluence of factors that led to my practical career. The pre-law course I took in college felt like a grown-up mixture of the writing and crossword puzzles I loved. I'd watched my mom struggle to support us after my dad left so it seemed irresponsible to move to New York City to try to get a job in writing or publishing. I scored well on the LSATs and when I was offered a scholarship to law school, I took it.

I could always write, I'd reasoned, but law school would be a backup plan should I ever really need to care for myself or a family. Three years of law school led to two years at a Boston firm, then ten years working part-time at a property management company while full-time raising a family. I stopped working as a lawyer in 2019 when the properties my company managed were sold. The same year, my youngest started kindergarten and I felt primed to find my second act.

With stable financial footing and my intense years of childrearing behind me, I could pursue the passions I'd let go. I became fierce on the tennis court, ratcheted up my crossword puzzling by tackling *The New York Times* each day, and began writing classes.

My exploration lasted eight weeks. In November, my husband sold his beer distribution business. Our expectations of being home together clashed. He envisioned us dropping the kids off at school, going out for a run and a coffee, then getting back in bed together. I had other plans: tennis every morning, lunch on the go, and writing in the library each afternoon. I was desperate to be alone, to create space for myself after so many years of being depleted by modern motherhood. The last weekend of February, I checked myself into a yoga and writing workshop in the Berkshires. I ate meals in silence, crossed the corridors in walking meditation, and journaled lists and musings.

Two weeks after my solo sojourn, the pandemic hit. Quarantine mocked my longing for independence. Instead, I landed a full-time gig as my daughter's kindergarten teacher, and as a full-service property manager (cooking, laundry, cleaning) for our five-person household.

By the end of March, my mother was battling COVID. States away, in Florida, she updated me daily with her digits: oxygen level, temperature, pulse. One morning, she hauntingly texted "I woke up." It was hard not to panic amid her precarious health and the virus's worldwide spread. By a stroke of fortune not afforded to so many, she miraculously recovered.

THAT SAME AWFUL WEEK, I noticed a Facebook group had formed in my Connecticut community to help address the shortage of masks for nurses and essential workers. I eyed the sewing machine that had been around since the last pandemic. I already baked challah for Shabbat and sourdough for gut health —why not add seamstress to my modern homesteading existence?

There was one problem. Save for the day it was profession-
ally tuned a decade ago, the Singer had never hummed in our
home. Eight years ago, when my son Ryan lost his first tooth, he
and I tried to use the machine to sew a pillow to hold it until the
tooth fairy arrived. We ended up with a tangled mess of loopy
threads. When my younger son Noah wanted to be a snowman
one Halloween, I tried again. I carefully guided the thread
through the catches but when I stepped on the pedal, the
stitches tangled until the top thread snapped. Stymied, I hand-
sewed snowy white fleece to a t-shirt and stuffed it to give him a
big belly. I traced his favorite pajamas and hand-stitched
matching fleece pants. When he tried them on, I ran wildly
around the house with a never-before and never-again seen "I
made pants" dance.

Now in quarantine, I felt bewildered by Katie, the 29-year-
old woman who had swiftly crafted a website to match requests
from frontline health care workers with volunteer sewists. I
couldn't get my kids to load their cereal bowls in the dishwasher,
yet Katie rallied strangers to donate, wash, iron, and cut fabric.
My patio was a pile of Amazon boxes needing recycling, hers
became a tidy clearinghouse for sewing supplies and mask
donations.

If Katie launched this effort while working and attending
graduate school, I decided I would at least try to figure out my
heirloom machine. Incredibly, I found YouTube videos of our
archaic Singer Red Eye, nicknamed for its exotic hand-painted
red ovals surrounding the gold logo. Those red eyes seemed to
lift, delighted, as I learned to fill a bobbin and thread a needle.
On FaceTime with a local sewing instructor, I learned to adjust
tension and to seal my stitches by planting my needle into the
fabric and rotating the entire piece of fabric 180 degrees, twice,
to close the seam.

And just like that, with about 20 minutes of virtual training, and oh yes, an unprecedented pandemic, Great-Grandma Sara's machine was back in action.

———

I WATCHED a dozen tutorials on the various mask designs, trying to make sense of which one would be most manageable for someone with a century-old machine and a seventh-grade home economics education. With pleats or without, elastic or ties, filter pocket or nose wire? After breakfast the next morning, Ryan, my then seventh grader, ironed my old quilting fabric while I continued down a dark hole of tutorials. He thumbed through the few pages of patterns I had printed, picked one up, and measured out a nine by seven rectangle.

"Wait...I'm not sure that's the one I want to use. There's this other video..." I trailed off, looking back at my phone to revisit the instructions.

Ryan kept cutting, then tossed two fabric pieces at me. "Mom, just go sew these together."

I did, grateful that my confident son had rescued me from the analysis paralysis that often plagued me. I'd known we were different this way. Me, researching recipes for hours when picking a chickpea curry to make for dinner and then running out of time to cook. Him, prone to jumping in without preparation, like spray painting a school project in new khakis and bare feet. I thought my overthinking meant I was applying myself. To me, his impulsiveness often looked like he wasn't trying hard enough and working on one activity while avoiding another. In that brief exchange in our kitchen, Ryan called out my procrastination and settled me in a chair behind that century-old machine.

———

TWO PROTOTYPES LATER, I signed up to make 20 masks for my town's food shelter. My first mask took an hour. Soon, I sewed four in that time. My stitch lines weren't perfect, but they were getting straighter. I delivered that first batch, another 20 to home health aides, and 25 kid-sized ones to our children's hospital.

I know I received a gift greater than my donations. I forged a connection among strangers and a purpose amid confinement. The Facebook group became a respite, full of troubleshooting, photographs of gorgeous masks, and banter about fabric favorites. We cheered on sewists in the 100-mask club, and incredibly, even some superstars who sewed a thousand. By summer, we used our mask scraps to create a giant quilt that memorializes our efforts and this moment in time.

I was too busy sewing (cooking, cleaning, and worrying) to bust into an "I made masks" dance. Yet each time my husband modeled my latest PPE, I felt the joy of that "I made pants" dance, glad for the opportunity to create something. When I needed it most, I found my time alone in a quiet corner of my basement, far from the grim infection tallies and the perpetual needs of my family. I spent hours escaping to a quiet corner of my basement. Audiobooks kept me company while I worked, like Elizabeth Gilbert's *City of Girls*, my book club's "not sad" pandemic selection. I delighted in its rash main character, Vivian Morris, fittingly, a costume designer and fashionista who sewed her way through New York City during World War II.

By summer, the group deemed its mission of outfitting essential workers complete and Katie's porch headquarters closed. My sewing time became a placeholder for me-time. I filled it with Zooming into writing classes, joining a critique group, and setting up my freelance website. I tackled each new assignment the way both Katie and Ryan would—by sitting in the chair and getting started.

BOTH OF THESE THINGS ARE TRUE

CAROLINE BERGER

This pandemic has been utter shit. And also the best time of my life. How can both of these things be true at the same time?

I'll let you in on a little secret, which I generally keep tucked under my hat because this is not the time to crow about personal growth. Amidst the soul-crushing awfulness of this pandemic, I have been quietly, personally, living out the happiest, most content, and most at-peace-with-my-demons period of my life.

My childhood best friend and next-door neighbor sent me a message a few months back: "You've basically been training for this your entire life, haven't you?"

Reader, I have. Certainly not intentionally—who on earth could have predicted that my middle years would include a global pandemic that keeps stretching on and on and on?—but, a few things about me: I am a lifelong, card-carrying introvert. Empath. Type 2 insomniac. Trauma survivor. Personality type INFP. I appreciate the quiet and being left alone.

First, though, the terrible, true thing. I work for a healthcare system in Baltimore, and every day I receive an email with daily COVID stats. Every other day in staff meetings, I discuss COVID with my colleagues. We sigh in frustration at the peaks in cases that follow every warm day or holiday. We have lost some of our own—doctors and staff with years of service under their belts. Our nurses are exhausted, mentally and physically. We keep scrambling for new ideas to reach our most vulnerable populations, including outfitting a mobile health clinic to take the vaccine to those with mobility or health issues that prevent them from going into a hospital. Every day I hear unbearable stories of sickness, grief, and loss. It is awful, and my heart breaks anew in an endless cycle.

On top of that, half of the work I do is centered around our violence intervention and prevention programs. Child sexual abuse, domestic violence, elder abuse, gun violence (Baltimore has had a yearly homicide rate above 300 for the past six years, and we are on track to hit that number again this year)—all exponentially worse and more challenging to address during a pandemic.

I am steeped in loss, sadness, and frustration.

ON SUNDAY, JANUARY 19, DANTE "TATER" Barksdale, the heart and soul of Safe Streets, a program of risky, on-the-ground violence interruption, a man who worked for more than a decade to keep Baltimore's streets safe from gun violence, was shot and killed. The entire city was stunned and in shock. My Safe Streets colleagues who worked with Dante for years were stunned and in shock. Our mayor, a personal friend of Dante, was stunned and in shock. As a city, we mourned, publicly and deeply.

This one hurt. A lot.

If you're not from Baltimore, you probably know it primarily from the phenomenally well-written HBO series, "The Wire," and the name Barksdale may ring a bell. Tater was the nephew of Nathan Barksdale, a Baltimore drug dealer who was purportedly one of the inspirations behind the character Avon Barksdale.

Tater was the best of us. Formed in the hard streets of East Baltimore, incarcerated, turned his life around and gave it willingly to the next generation of at-risk young men battling systemic racism, economic blight, and generations of thug life as the most viable career option. He was the guy in the bright orange Safe Streets t-shirt trying to keep the peace. When Grace Kearney, who co-authored his memoir *Growing Up Barksdale: A True Baltimore Story*, asked about one of his "kids" who had gotten involved in a shooting, on either side of the gun, he would say, "That's just his trauma. Let me tell you who he really was."

He saw people. Really and truly saw them.

A convert to Islam while in prison, he said, when asked if he ever talked to God, "God is in social encounters. I talk to him all the time."

Kids in Baltimore—or at least kids who grow up in what author Lawrence Brown dubbed the "Black Butterfly" neighborhoods—know what to do when they hear gunshots. As opposed to kids from the "White L" neighborhoods, a patch of White gentrification stretching along the waterfront and up the column of downtown, dotted by the wealth of Johns Hopkins campuses and hospitals of this historically hypersegregated, majority Black city. They lose dozens of friends before graduating high school. Young men in particular live with the knowledge that, if they make it past the age of 30, they are one of the lucky few.

One young man, Devon Little, was gunned down this spring a little after one a.m. on March 25 in Southwest Baltimore, right at that magic age of 30. His life was cut short not only after surviving two previous near-fatal gunshot wounds (the first during a surge in violence in 2015 after the arrest and death of Freddie Gray from injuries suffered in police custody; the second in a 2016 shooting spree that also injured an eight-year-old girl), but on the very block where, five years ago, police falsely accused him of murder. He was convicted and sentenced to a life in prison, but later acquitted in a second trial; there was conflicting witness testimony and no physical evidence to tie him to the shooting. That kind of thing happens a lot here. Devon worked for Meals on Wheels doing food prep. He had a young daughter, loved music, and wrote and recorded rap songs in the home studio his mother created for him in her basement in hopes that it would keep him home, and safe.

He is one of 175 people killed in Baltimore so far this year, six months in.

Devon, and so many others—those were Tater's kids.

Those were the ones he died to save.

He once said, "The most gangster shit of all is forgiveness."

To honor his life and his work, we had to grieve for him, but we also had to forgive his killer. We had to make damned sure none of his "kids" took the easy route of payback for his death.

On May 20, police announced that they had arrested a suspect in connection to his murder. And on June 19, Juneteenth, the city of Baltimore named the corner of North Caroline and East Fayette Streets "The Dante Way" to honor his life and legacy.

BUT BACK TO JANUARY, 2021. That's it, right? After Dante's murder, after all of the loss that had come before it, it couldn't possibly get any worse. We are maxed out on grief at this point. Our hearts are pandemic-weary and broken into a million pieces by the violence that has not ceased during this time of general isolation.

Gunshots still ring out every night.

That wasn't it. Not by a longshot.

Sometimes irony is a real motherfucker.

MY COLLEAGUE, Lori, came to work with our team a few years ago. After an early career in public relations and raising two kids, she was ready to do something that felt like giving back to the community, and became executive assistant to our director of violence intervention and prevention programs.

The morning of Saturday, January 30, Kenneth Gerstley, Lori's husband of more than twenty years, was going about his normal workday for an ATM company he ran with some of his siblings. He had just refilled an ATM at a local convenience store and was returning to his car.

He was gunned down in the parking lot.

Shot dead.

They didn't even take any money from him or go inside to rob the store.

Somehow, working on issues of violence prevention, one thinks that violence cannot touch you. You know all of the signs to look out for. You know what to avoid. You are unshockable in the face of the unspeakably awful things that humans intentionally do to other humans.

But the very existence of random acts of violence cuts right through that tough skin and strips away that flimsy, paper-thin "this will never happen to me" illusion.

Ken is survived by his wife and two daughters, siblings, parents, an entire community. He was the guy that made everyone laugh, asked you about your day, gave the best hugs. "A big teddy bear," is how loved ones described him.

How could all of that joy and love just disappear in one single moment?

I still don't know.

Months later, I am still mulling over how to express my condolences to my colleague.

I have no words.

I always have words, even when I have nothing else to offer the world.

Not this time.

GRIEF IS MY CONSTANT COMPANION. I am afloat in an ocean of loss. I have been watching my friends lose elderly parents and beloved friends to COVID and other illnesses. One friend contracted COVID early on, recovered, nursed his dying father until his last days, then, months later, did the same for his stepmother. In April, I helped him fill a moving truck with the last of their worldly possessions, stopping every now and then to talk him down from a panic attack, rub his back, touch a tiny square of the back of his neck with one finger (because we were both not yet vaccinated and still bumbling around in masks, keeping ourselves six feet apart). That was the first human skin other than my own that I had touched since March 2020.

BUT GRIEF IS LARGER, even, than that. This special mix of pandemic grief and built-up White rage.

I have—we all have—been witness to and participants in the collective outrage against:

Police violence.

The killing of activists.

The exhausting, brutal cycle of murders of people of color for being a color that is not white.

Mass shootings.

More mass shootings.

More. Fucking. Mass shootings.

Femicide.

The storming of our capitol.

All the White supremacist residue of the Trump years that is still, to this day, sparking hateful, bigoted, racist, misogynistic attacks.

Grief is also smaller. So tiny we breathe it in with every breath, can't wash it off of our skin.

I have been witness, in particular, to the unbearably heavy burdens of my female friends balancing work, home school, unhelpful spouses, and caregiving for parents.

The weight of it all is crushing.

Every.

Single.

Day.

Now for the other true thing, the good thing. My personal history is also utter shit, but I have spent the past two decades righting my ship, reinforcing the holes in my life raft with resiliency, mindfulness, meditation, deep trauma processing, and healing.

In the face of all this loss, I find that I have intangible things to offer my friends: a non-judgmental listening ear, advice when asked for, tips for staying healthy, mini pep-talks.

It feels good to feel useful.

My heart is full at being gifted the ability to give something, anything, in this time of so much being taken from us.

Dozens of friends, some I haven't heard from in years, have messaged me to thank me for a social media post that hit home for them, or to ask me how to deal with the utter shit, or to just reconnect.

HOW CAN both of these things be true?

The bad thing: everything we thought we knew about everything has been ripped to shreds.

I am endlessly heartbroken over what we have been through together these past sixteen months and will keep going through for who knows how much longer.

The good thing: everything we thought we knew about everything has been ripped to shreds.

I am endlessly grateful, and filled with hope for the future.

I RECENTLY SCORED some essays for the Baldwin Prize, a local essay competition for ninth graders at Baltimore City College High School, created by an alum of the school. I have been doing this for a few years now, but this year was different.

The prompt was for them to write about someone they knew who had managed to maintain communication with someone far away during the pandemic. They were to interview them, then write the essay either from their own perspective or the perspective of their interviewee.

In a normal year, the essays are usually interesting, sometimes heartbreaking, and often funny and reflective, but also flawed in ways that ninth-grade essays are flawed. With a scoring rubric up to 30 points, generally the essays I get fall in the 15-20 range.

This year was different. I was blown away. Two utterly perfect 30-pointers; two just below, at 28.

The kids are alright.

They are going to be okay.

Someday.

Somehow.

SOMEHOW, we get through this.

Someday, we move into a better future.

Carrying our griefs on our weary fucking shoulders.

Squirreling away small joys like so many acorns.

Both of these things can be true.

Acorns can become trees.

Somehow, we get through this.

THIS ESSAY IS DEDICATED to the city of Baltimore, and to the memories of Dante Barksdale, Kenneth Gerstley, and all of the lives we lost as a result of both COVID-19 and community violence.

SEASONS

SHARI WINSLOW

My last day of teaching inside a classroom happened on a Friday back in March 2020. Thin snowflakes drifted over the parking lot in the gray afternoon as we carried armloads to our cars. Some of my colleagues took their document cameras and extra monitors. I brought home my school laptop and an extra copy of the novel I thought I might still teach in May. As an afterthought, I grabbed an extra canister of Clorox wipes I'd tucked into the dusty corner cabinet back in August. A week earlier, we'd been told we would hold our spring conferences via phone; now schools were closed until April 27. As I drove to pick up my own children, praying my daughter remembered to bring home her PE clothes, I thought about the strange juxtaposition of snowflakes and cherry blossoms, already beginning to bloom.

———

I WATCHED school districts around the country launch into distance learning. Wealthier districts could ensure access to technology and the internet almost instantly; my district announced that we wouldn't provide for a few what we couldn't provide for everyone. We didn't hold Zoom classes or require work. Our philosophy was "Do No Harm." Teachers spent the last two weeks in March calling our families through Google Voice, so we didn't have to use our personal numbers. I emailed my seniors: *I really want to check in with all of you and make sure you're okay, so I'll be calling all of you. It's going to show up on your phones as some random number you won't recognize, but please let me know what time of day is best so you're expecting it. If you'd rather have me send a text or leave a message, let me know that too.* My principal insisted that we phone, but my kids were much more receptive to texting. Still, some of them answered.

"How are you doing, seriously?"

"I'm a little anxious."

Six weeks later, we handed out Chromebooks in the bus loop and hosted weekly Zooms, with different subjects assigned to each day. I met with my classes on Monday mornings, then collapsed on the couch after lunch. I didn't know how exhausting it would be, to project all of my teaching energy through a screen while I sat at my dining room table.

On the last day before the closure, before any of us understood that we wouldn't be back in April, I told my kids to finish reading the novel we were studying.

"You've got nothing but time, right?" I joked—before I thought about how many would take on extra hours at Dominos or Taco Bell because they needed the money more than they needed my class.

I started taking long walks at dawn, listening to podcasts. When I walked by my son's school on Monday mornings, I watched families line up to pick up five days' worth of meals from masked and gloved volunteers—food their kids would normally eat at school, and food they wouldn't have at home.

TEACHING in 2020 ended in snow and began again in fire. The sky filled with smoke over Labor Day weekend, and on Monday night, the winds picked up and wildfires from eastern Washington rushed in. We lost power in the middle of the night. Tossing around in an uneasy sleep, I woke for good when the fan in our bedroom went silent. I laid in the sweaty darkness, the air outside too toxic for open windows. I checked my phone but couldn't get a signal, couldn't read my email. Just after six o'clock in the morning, I learned through a text chain with my colleagues that the first day of school had been postponed. The robocall from the district followed a few minutes later, and after that, my phone died.

"This is our new Snow Day," I said to my husband, "with absolutely none of the joy." I crawled back into bed and dozed while he drove a few miles to a Starbucks that had power and a long line of cars.

The power flickered on sometime after lunch, and I opened up my laptop to finish my district-directed orientation slides.

The next morning, determined to document the day, I donned my spirit wear and herded the kids into the driveway for our traditional First Day of School pictures. We smiled through the smoke under a yellow sky, then trudged back inside to log on to our computers.

MY DAUGHTER BEGAN her first year of high school from a desk in her bedroom; my son began his last year of elementary school from a desk in his. It's difficult not to grieve this loss. For ten years I've trusted our neighborhood elementary school with my babies, and my heart breaks at the thought that our very last year there might be entirely remote. I think of what we'll miss: Family Art Night, Battle of the Books, PTA movie nights, Dance-a-thons, the teacher-hosted holiday dinner before Winter Break.

My daughter knew no one at her new school when she signed on for her first class. The week before school started, the district told us we were not to use the Breakout Rooms on Zoom because it didn't allow for adequate supervision. As a teacher of literature, discussions are the heartbeat of my class. I've never been a great lecturer, and my school values student-centered learning. The thought of talking at a bunch of black boxes every day, all day was demoralizing. Teachers debated this on the union Facebook page. We can't hear every conversation at once in our actual classrooms when we're checking in with different groups, either, and we understand the importance of establishing norms.

One teacher said, "Well, to be fair, when we were in breakout rooms during the district training days, there was an awful lot of off-task side talk."

"Side talk is okay—and frankly necessary," I replied. "Kids need to make connections with each other, too."

OUR DAY GOES LIKE THIS: I wake up early—almost early enough to go for a walk before I need to get ready for class, except that my son wakes up shortly after I do and doesn't like to be awake and alone. The walk can wait.

My husband stays up late and wakes up last, but the coffee is brewing by 7:30.

By 8:00, our daughter is logged into her first class of the day, my husband is finishing his giant bowl of oatmeal with blueberries and flax, and our son is ready to log in as well. His class doesn't start until 9:00, but he is at his best in the morning, ready to go. His teacher will often let him into class early, but she says "Hey, Kiddo, I'm still working on planning, okay?"

"It's all good," he tells her, and he works on his reading for the day.

My children disappear into their rooms, and I send a silent prayer of thanks that they are old enough to manage this on their own. My friends with young kids struggle, and I understand. But the data from our district surveys shows that the families most upset about remote learning are white—those who don't bear the burden of the highest COVID rates. Who often have the privilege of working from home. Who are less likely to spread the virus in multigenerational households.

My husband is a software engineer who works from the study. I want to make sure the kids have a designated work space, too, so I set up their compact IKEA desks and Office Depot stacking drawers in their rooms. I set up my teaching station at the dining room table once again and tell my husband he'd damn well better clean up after he sautés his breakfast kale and potatoes. This is my classroom now.

Our son's class ends shortly before mine. He tiptoes out of his bedroom and mouths, "Are you on mute?"

"Yeah, baby, they're in breakout rooms. Let's do fish sticks for lunch. Can you preheat the oven?"

As soon as I say goodbye to my sophomores—waving, smiling, reminding them that I'll be in open office hours for asynchronous support until 2:30—I scoop the fish sticks onto plates. My husband doles out carrot sticks or broccoli, and I warm up last night's sweet potato and black bean enchiladas. I push aside my laptop, and the four of us eat together. And it occurs to me that while nothing about this is normal, some of these moments are still sweet. And someday, when I look back on this time, I'll think of this, too.

———

THESE DAYS, I begin class by letting a handful of kids into my Zoom room, a few at a time. It's important to greet each of them by name, even if all I see is their name against a black box.

"Morning, Kim! Hi, Maria! Good to see you, Gabe!"

Even as I say it, I laugh to myself, because all I see is a name in white letters against a black screen. But Gabe types in the chat box: "Hi, Ms. Winslow!"

"Hey, Christina! Hi, Lena! Good morning, Emmanuel! While I'm letting everyone in, tell me one thing you did this weekend to take care of yourself. Pop it into the chat. Meredith, you got a puppy? I want to see her! Seriously, can we see her? Oh, gosh, she's so cute! Hi, Eliza!"

Sometimes I ask, "What's the best takeout in Federal Way?" I take attendance while they type. Panda Express! Olive Garden! Taco Bell!

"You guys are making me hungry and I'm sorry I asked," I lie. But I also smile, because 16-year-old me probably would have voted for Panda Express too.

"What if I want really good pho?" I ask them.

"My house, sorry," one girl replies immediately. "But since you can't come over, the place by Barnes and Noble is actually pretty good."

I only have 55 minutes with them. Maybe that's too much. Mostly it feels like not enough.

I steal an idea from one of my colleagues: one-on-one check-ins during afternoon office hours, or "Asynchronous Time." They sign up on a Google doc and choose a question to talk about: *What's the best book you've ever read? What's one small thing that makes your day better? Describe your relation-ship with your parents or siblings. What's one thing you find really annoying? If you could have lunch with one person, living or dead, who would it be?* I beg them to show up and promise not to take more than five minutes of their time. During those check-ins, most of them turn on their cameras. Some of them allow me into their bedrooms or the corners of their living room. Two of them log in outside, and one hunkers down in a garage because, he says, it's just quieter. One girl cradles a weeping toddler while a young boy plays with toys in the background. She loves *Pride and Prejudice* and *Jane Eyre* and Shirley Jackson, and we both grin when I say I also loved *The Haunting of Hill House,* and isn't it a great, cozy fall read?

I've never been in a room with this student, but two weeks later she sends me an email: *I find your class so interesting. It's been awhile since I've found a curriculum that changed me. This class challenges me in a way that is both engaging and thought-provoking.*

Her email brings tears to my eyes, though, because I understand that these five-minute connections are more impor-tant than any lesson I could ever teach.

—

IT SNOWED OVER PRESIDENTS' Day weekend. Western Washington is good for about one significant "snow event" each year, and mid-February is often when we'll have a Snow Day or two. When snow hit the forecast earlier in the week, students wanted to know: Would we still have Snow Days, even though we were doing school from home?

Many of us thought that we should still give our kids that small gift: the romance of a Snow Day. That the pandemic had taken enough. But official district communication dashed that hope, and our principal followed up with an email to make sure we understood that school would continue even if we lost power or staff who still taught from their empty classrooms couldn't safely make it in. We would have to call in an absence if we couldn't teach remotely.

"If it starts to snow during class," I told my juniors, "I'll take my laptop into the backyard and teach in the snow. Maybe it'll make you pay attention if I'm cold and outside, and also, it will remind us all of what it's like when you all see two snowflakes through the window and lose your minds."

At the end of class on Friday, the sky was heavy but the ground was bare. I hadn't lost hope.

"I know it'll snow," I said. "I can smell it. Your only homework is to enjoy the snow like little children."

We had 12 inches between Friday night and Sunday afternoon. My family slogged through unplowed streets to sled down the small hill next to the field at the middle school. Later, I took a walk through the park near the elementary school, the silence as thick as the snow. At home, we made hot chocolate and homemade pizza, and even though my New Year's resolution was to establish better boundaries between work and home when the same walls contained it all, something made me log into my laptop on Saturday night. I smiled to see an email from one of my students.

Good morning, Ms. Winslow! THE SNOW WE WISHED FOR CAME! I'm kind of sad we didn't get to see you in class sitting in the middle of all this snow, but I just wanted to share my excitement! I hope you enjoy the weekend! I'll definitely be getting my homework done.

By Monday afternoon, the snow shifted to rain. The snowmen sagged; the snow tunnel collapsed. My son opened the door to gaze sadly at the soggy remnants of his hard work.

"Sorry, Buddy," I said. "But we had fun."

He turned around and said, "It kind of smells like spring out there."

So it does.

In a few days, all traces of snow will vanish into the wet lawn. The air is sweet with the first breath of spring. I never feel the need to crawl up, crawl out from winter's quiet depths until I smell it, that singing fresh scent under the mud, under the earth and the grass. It's almost painful, that first gasp of sharp sweet air, like a birth, like a death.

I don't know what the future will bring, or what teaching will look like, even after we return to the classroom. But I know that in just a few weeks, the cherry blossoms will bloom again and burst over the sidewalks, as soft as snow.

VIEW FROM THE COURTYARD

MARIE HOLMES

When I was a child, I spent countless hours mucking around in my backyard, making potions and mud pies, lost in an imaginative universe devoid of any adult presence. I was an orphan, a princess, a pioneer. And, as I explained to my son when he requested that we move to a "country house" like Grandma's (in the city of Portland, Oregon), I always dreamed of living one day in New York City.

He didn't miss a beat.

"And now look," he said. "It's boring!"

To me, of course, it's not boring. You can uncover every corner of the world in New York if you know where to look and how to listen.

But my ten-year-old longed for a backyard of his own, and a dog to romp through the grass with him.

I reminded him that we did have a small green space—four corners of gangly shrubs crisscrossed in asphalt—between the different wings of our apartment building. That was more than most city dwellers got.

"It's not the same," he said.

This past Christmas, against my better judgment, all logic, and the terms of our lease, we brought home a puppy.

Then in March, everything went on pause and, in our indefinite hibernation, the courtyard and the puppy became the only real world that remained.

The children were initially ecstatic when the schools closed, and those first days home had the flavor of snow cancellations—temporary treats sprinkled with movies and hot chocolate.

Then we started losing count of how many days it had been, and, one morning, my six-year-old daughter pulled me behind her bedroom door. I kneeled down, and she cupped her hands to whisper into my ear. She'd had a bad dream, she said. A really bad one.

What happened?

Donald Trump killed Mommy.

I held her close, promising that I would never let him, and I would never leave her.

The narrative didn't surprise me. Since the day in early November 2016, when she discovered me hiding crouched in the bathroom, weeping, watching Kate McKinnon sing "Hallelujah," he has been the cartoon villain of her world. The only person who'd ever made Mommy cry.

What took me aback was how much of our fear she had quietly absorbed. While we'd been making cupcakes and playing charades and staying up late like this was all a big slumber party, it hadn't escaped her that something sinister was behind the sudden turning of the whole world outside in.

We tried to reassure her with extra hugs and I love yous. But the next day, fishing in a junk drawer, she found a spare smoke alarm battery and asked me what it was. Suddenly, she was full of uncharacteristically anxious questions. Was there going to be a fire? How would we get out onto the fire escape with all those bars on the window? How many blocks away was the nearest fire station?

There wasn't going to be a fire, I said. But her faith in my certainty had been shaken.

Later, she told my wife: "Mom, just in case—I love you."

While our one directive is to stay home, we have, since day one, found that by a certain hour of the afternoon there is no quantity of screen time that can soothe us, and we slowly organize ourselves: shoes, keys—such a process!—and trample outside.

In the beginning, we took them to the nearby park, but then the yellow signs went up announcing that the playgrounds weren't sterile, and then the red signs went up and the playground gates were all chained and locked indefinitely.

We decided early on to expand our "immediate family" to include neighbors in the building who also have a ten-year-old. We figured that earlier play dates had cross-contaminated us already, and were eager for some ballast to see us through this.

So we began meeting in the courtyard in the afternoons, after the dissolution of the virtual school day. The three children found long sticks and other treasures in the neglected garden, and were soon happily chasing each other about, the puppy trailing at their heels.

On the day of my daughter's bad dream, I was leaning against a brick wall in a narrow band of sunlight while the kids darted from one corner of the yard to another. At one point I took out my phone to check the news. Moments later, my son ran up to me.

"The chief needs to see you," he said. He led me behind a shrub. Naively, I stepped right across a patch of dirt.

"You have to knock on the door first!" he reprimanded me.

I was granted entry on my second attempt. My six-year-old

was perched regally atop a plastic shopping cart stuffed with a baby blanket, a jump rope, and some other pink miscellany.

"Guard," she addressed me, her head high, her voice assured. "What is that?"

"My phone?"

She instructed me to hand it over, tossed it into the bed of the cart, and sat right back down on top of it.

Another official was dispatched to return me to my post, where I was informed, some minutes later, that the chief was not going to dismiss me outright, but she was going to retain possession of my phone.

Back in my spot of sunlight, without my phone to distract me, I marveled at how in their game they had determined that the littlest and least powerful among them would get to be the leader, as though they all tacitly understood how badly she needed a sense of control over the spinning world.

In the days following, they built a fort out of bits of wood debris rescued from the garbage area and repurposed an old intercom as spy equipment. They even found a worthy villain in the building's super, who asked us not to use the hose or step on any of the plants. They hollered a daily code word if one of them saw him coming.

COVID-19 somehow turned my city-dwelling, digital natives into the rapscallions of yore, scampering through narrow alleyways with their little dog scurrying behind them.

I still don't know how, collectively, we're going to make it through this, nor do I have any idea what the other side looks like. But I have learned, watching these children navigate this tiny courtyard, listening to the ambulance sirens wailing past, that if we give ourselves over to our imaginations, we may find the stories that will heal us.

LITTLE EARTHQUAKES: WHEN
FRIENDSHIPS FRACTURE

LAUREL HILTON

COVID-19 has asked a lot of our society: to stay six feet apart, to wear a mask, to shelter-in-place, to cancel birthdays, vacations, and holiday plans. It has required us to be patient when patience is like standing in a mile-long bathroom line at your favorite concert—feeling like you will never make it to relief.

COVID has made me hyper-aware of my family's safety and terrified that my parents and older relatives will get sick, or worse, lose their lives to this awful virus.

But one thing I never expected from COVID's wrath was a crack in a friendship that I have held sacred for most of my life.

THIS PANDEMIC DIDN'T CREATE the divisions that have caused stress between family and friends—politics has handled that efficiently on its own. The last four years have been corrosive, chaotic, and divisive. But my friend and I have weathered it all. Sure, we've had our different opinions over the years; that's part of what's made our friendship successful and long-lasting. We never shy away from hard truths or standing up for what we believe in. I love her fiercely for her opinions. I know that she feels the same for me. But I'm not sure how she truly feels about my own cautious response to the virus.

When COVID caught the world by surprise, we held out hope that it wouldn't get too bad, that it would last a few weeks or maybe a month. A year later, and it continues to gallop across the globe, insidiously unleashing new variants to keep us isolated from each other. Similarly, little fissures emerged in my friendship, slowly eating away at the foundation we carefully created and nurtured for decades. It became a crack in our relationship that I didn't recognize until it was nearly too late.

I HAVE ALWAYS BEEN a rule follower. If my teacher said, "Turn in your homework on Friday," I did. If my parents said to be home by 10 p.m., I was. Now, if my boss says, "Finish this project before you go home," I do. If a recipe calls for exactly two tablespoons of olive oil, you better believe there are only two tablespoons of oil in the meal.

I also trust science. Since the U.S. lockdown began in March 2020, and throughout the slow crawl toward re-opening in the spring of 2021, the Center for Disease Control has been my go-to guidance counselor. I listen to doctors like Anthony Fauci, to scientists, bioethicists, and virologists. I worship objectivity, logic, and intuition.

Though I hold a master's degree in journalism, I avoid the network news as much as possible, knowing that no matter whether the newscast leans right or left, it sensationalizes the pandemic and scares me out of my wits.

Like a large swath of Americans, I have refrained from seeing my parents, other relatives, and friends. I've isolated my kids and Zoomed for work until my eyes ache from staring at a screen for ten hours a day. More than a year later, I still haven't been face-to-face with more than a dozen people at a time, and always outdoors.

Above all, I have tried to remain calm, compassionate, and open-minded in the face of opposition to my views. While I often have strong opinions, I don't usually force them on others. "To each her own," I'd say in pre-COVID times. However, I was surprised that someone who shared my upbringing, outlook, and philosophy on life would think so differently about the pandemic.

THE FIRST GLIMMER of a fracture in our friendship surfaced in June 2020, when the pandemic became very real for me. Another friend of mine lost his otherwise healthy mother to COVID. She was in her 70s, but so is my mom and she's in good health. I mentioned the loss to my friend, and she didn't seem dismayed by the effect it had on me. She shrugged it off *as these things just happen*, which I took to mean that if my mom had died of COVID, my friend (who knows my mom) might pass it off as something fleeting and mildly unfortunate. Whether that was true or not, the idea stung.

Later in the summer, my friend and I went camping together with a small group of families. I was hesitant to go, but my family and I missed the outdoors and I figured that we'd have our own tents, food, and gear. And it would be safe enough.

But it wasn't.

My friend, her family members, and many others in attendance shared food buffet-style and sat knee-to-knee around the campfire. Yes, they had masks, but they hung below their noses, cupping their chins like tiny hammocks. I felt awkward and wondered if I was overreacting. My friends are knowledgeable; perhaps they realized something I didn't. I regretted going and began to think maybe I didn't know my friend as well as I thought.

In October 2020, with the election looming ahead of us, people were anxious, no matter who they wanted in the White House. Sitting outdoors at our favorite café, over coffee and croissants on a mild day, a conversation with my friend turned to personal rights and conspiracy theories—two issues I never imagined talking about in unison, and not with my rational, intelligent friend.

Personal rights have never crossed my mind with this pandemic. People didn't choose to be exposed to a deadly virus. We didn't ask for a disaster of this magnitude to sweep in and upset our way of life. But one thing we could choose was how to protect ourselves and others. For me, it's a matter of the greater good: I protect you; you protect me. We get through it together. I'm not a fan of government intervention in our daily lives, but I also recognize that the government provides us with many benefits. I didn't see COVID-19 safety guidelines as an infringement upon my rights. My friend's take: "The government can't tell me what to do."

When 9/11 happened, our country was forever changed. We had to take off our shoes and jackets in airport security lines and dump perfectly good bottles of water in the trash before entering the terminal. It sucked. It still sucks 20 years later. But we do it because we want to fly to visit family, travel for work, or take a vacation. We want to protect ourselves and each other. Do the right thing. Follow the rules. My friend heard me out, but replied quickly that it was "overkill." She admonished, "The pandemic was blown out of proportion by the media and was just like any other flu season."

Because I don't watch the network news or read much

online media, I have largely avoided talk of conspiracy theories before that fall day at the cafe with my friend. Yet I was amazed to learn that my friend had read up on many of them, and possibly believed a few. At that moment, I wanted to stop time, wrap our friendship in a cocoon or place it in a time capsule that had an "open at a future date" sticker to prevent exposing its fragility to more of the divisive and bitter social side effects of COVID.

AS WOMEN GET OLDER, we often shed friendships like clothes in our closets. The hot pink angora sweater from 1996 is a little too snug across the chest now and rides up your midriff. The cute little black dress from 2003 doesn't fit in all the right places anymore. And that's ok. As we age, we change. Our friends change. But what about the friendship that is like your favorite pair of jeans? The ones that fit you through college, the birth of your children, and perimenopause. They are weathered and comfortable as hell. You want to keep them just as they are, forever. Even if they rip or fray or tear at the seams, you'd never consider discarding them.

Before COVID, I never imagined any opinion, remark, belief, or act would threaten what my friend and I shared. Never had I ever questioned if my friend would be someone with whom I'd have to consider parting ways.

IN JANUARY 2021, we casually debated the term "essential employees:" who they were, who they weren't, and whether they should be offered special protections. Our conversation found me defending groups of people my friend had championed in the past: those who are less fortunate, have reduced access to medical care, those who risk their lives daily to help others. She was adamant. I was mystified. At this point, I kind of shut down. I realized then that nothing I could say about precautions for this unprecedented virus were going to change her mind. I side-stepped into a discussion about the media response debate—one area where we stood on common ground.

And then came the discussion about vaccines. It comes as no surprise that I will get a COVID vaccine. I follow rules. I believe in science. A vaccine brings the promise of gathering with friends and family in real life. Soon, I hope.

Will my friend get the vaccine? She isn't sure. Part of me doesn't want to know what she decides. I want to understand and respect her opinions. And I want to sustain this friendship, which despite everything that has transpired this past year, I still cherish. It's worth preserving and smoothing over the cracks until the foundation is once again firm.

BEFORE AND AFTER

LEA GROVER

"We are not new at this." Somehow that phrase is supposed to comfort, but it does not. Rather, it exhausts. We are not new at avoiding illness, we are not new at avoiding people, we are not new at existential dread.

The day before the lockdown begins, my phone rings. It's the hospital, telling me that due to new virus protocol, a phrase that will soon vanish to be replaced by "cover restrictions," they are postponing my husband's surgery by three days. This will be his fourth brain surgery for glioblastoma, the most aggressive form of brain cancer. It has been 12.5 years since the first, though the average survival is only 16 months. It is only six months since the third surgery, during which he suffered a stroke. Our children still cry as I hold them at bedtime sometimes, asking why we can't go back to "normal," when Daddy will be like he was before the surgery, the only surgery they remember, before the stroke took his left side and our lives began to change indisputably for the worse. They have been excused from school the next day, Friday the 13th, and we do not know when they will return.

AS THE PANDEMIC PROGRESSES, we live in a separate, pocket universe of terror and chaos. I have hidden myself inside the hospital despite these new restrictions, and in order not to be trapped away from my husband when he is so ill, I stay inside his room. I often think of Anne Frank's family with shame. I am not permitted here. If caught, I will be forced to leave him here, surrounded by terrified doctors and nurses who smile behind ever-growing arrays of donated PPE, but whose eyes count the sick, and the dead. I am in greater danger here, to be certain, but the idea of leaving this tiny room—the horrid chair that twists my spine as I snatch an hour of sleep here or there, as I prop my laptop on my knees and put on the same fake smile and Skype my children that "Daddy is getting better, Daddy is getting better, Daddy is getting better"—sounds like a death sentence. He is not getting better. He is throwing clots into his legs and lungs. The hospital lobby is full of coughing, terrified Chicagoans. The street outside is transformed by tents for testing. On the far side of the tents is my sister's apartment, and I look towards her window and imagine she can see me when I wave.

A MONTH into the pandemic we return home to the children, a subdued if joyful reunion. The next day we learn my sister, across the street from the hospital, was found dead in her apartment, presumably of COVID-19. There are not enough tests for the dead, and we will never know for certain. I wrap myself in as much makeshift gear as I can to mimic the hospital staff, and drive to identify her corpse. I am told that this is the weekend the state will have to begin running the crematoriums around the clock. It takes six hours to reduce a human to ashes, I am told. There are only so many ovens.

"We are not new at this," I think, remembering the last time I was at a social gathering among friends. Two months ago, though it feels like an eternity, one of my dearest friends died from a heart attack. She was pregnant. The baby did not survive.

My friends are making bread. They are taking walks. They are learning to work remotely. They are frustrated about all the things their children are "missing out on." My children are watching their father wince but joke when I give him his twice-daily injections of blood thinners. My children are watching him lose his perception of objects on his left. My children are watching the ambulance out their window as it carries their father away on a stretcher to identify further bleeding in his brain, for more surgeries. My children are watching me sit in my pajamas with the phone to my ear, mourning their aunt, calming their father, managing his healthcare from a distance. My children are watching me cry in between their Zoom classes.

Every other week it is another thing. This is true of the news, but more so in my house. The president has told people to inject bleach. My husband has a pulmonary embolism. New York has begun digging mass graves in the park. My husband begins radiation and suffers brain necrosis. A nursing home in Italy is found full of dead bodies. My husband loses the ability to climb the stairs to our bedroom, and we rent a hospital bed. Everybody I know sends me links to celebrity videos of "good news," Doctor Who hiding in a closet and telling the children they'll be okay, teachers around the country creating wholesome content. My children learn to help their father play simple games, keep him on task, let him "cheat" so that they can enjoy this time. They know they are doing it, and he does not.

Our youngest turns eight without a birthday party. I am not

even there. I am with her father at the hospital again. When we decided to have children, I told myself, "If he lives until they're eight, they'll remember him, they'll know him." A week after her birthday I bundle their father into the car and tell them, "Say goodbye to Daddy and tell him you love him, I don't know if he'll come home this time." He does. It is not the last time I tell them this.

We are not new at this.

The deaths keep coming. Colleagues. Friends. Children. None over the age of forty. The number of dead people in my phone continues to grow, and my husband continues to rally from each setback...but not quite enough. He has another brain surgery, alone this time, and I begin leaving the house after dark, driving for hours, going nowhere, chain-smoking cigarettes because why the fuck not when the world is ending. The world doesn't end, though. We surpass a million Americans dead, but not my husband. He is still there. I buy a pool for the kids, and they splash joyfully in the water as their father watches through the window. He cannot go to the yard, his world is shrinking. He is shrinking. He and I are both down about thirty pounds. Thirty-five. Forty.

I start to plan for the "after." To go to work in a world where I am without him, where we are all reentering physical spaces full of fear and confusion and gratitude. That I can feel gratitude is the greatest kindness the year offers me. I am grateful for so much. I am constantly grateful. My sister is dead and my husband is dying and I am brought to tears nearly every day by what I have. My husband at home, with his children, playing broken games, and losing his sense of taste and everything to his left. Restricted to the first floor and a wheelchair.

My sister's birthday passes, but she remains the same age. Our twins turn 11, and my husband begins to get sicker, fast. He is in the hospital every few days for falls, fevers, strokes. He needs catheters every six hours, which I do for him. I would do anything for him, and he knows this, even the undignified things like making his life painful and frustrating with needles and tubes. Again there is no birthday party, but I get my flu shot, and that's something. Trump gets COVID. The COVID deaths are compared to a 9/11 every day. We fill out our absentee ballots and I drop them in a box, wondering if my husband will survive to see the results. A week after the election, I'm still wondering. Another dear friend dies, also of a sudden stroke, likely caused by COVID. I watch the funeral on Zoom, his young widow shoveling dirt on the grave as is the Jewish custom. I sit shiva with her in my little rectangle on the monitor. We are not new at this.

The country mourns a pandemic holiday season. Thanksgiving and Channukah are subdued affairs. He is having a stroke a week. His appetite is failing, as is his strength. He begins hospice on Christmas Eve. I buy myself presents for him to give me. I wrap them. I open them in front of him, and he is delighted by my reaction. He believes he has managed this task on his own.

Five people are dead after an insurgency in the Capitol, and my husband follows them. One week later my state expands vaccine eligibility to include family members who are caregivers for people with a list of conditions, including cancer and epilepsy. I don't know this at the time, of course, but when I learn, I sign up for my shot. My husband donates his brain to the hospital, to the research teams, so that other glioblastoma patients might someday expect the 13.5 years he had. With his brain removed, the hospital returns my husband to the funeral home. The funeral home transfers him to the crematorium. I know how long it will take to get his ashes back. I'm not new at this. Only now it is "I," not "we."

Nobody can hug me. They send "hugs" on Zoom, and

through text, and over the phone. "You're not alone," they say. But the words "alone together" hover in the air. We have all been so alone, all year. It's been ten months since the country shut down. COVID is the third leading cause of death for 2020, cancer is second.

Everything is changed. Everything is unfamiliar, from "family time" that consists only of me and my children, to the changing weather and the ability to stand outside the house and watch the trees bud. I don't know how to talk to people. I don't even know what I like to do. I have not had fun since my husband's stroke, nearly two years ago, and I have not attempted to cultivate hobbies on my own for nearly 14 years.

My number comes up, and I make my appointment to join Team Pfizer. As the pharmacist rolls up my sleeve and prepares the injection, I begin to cry. I start to apologize and she waves my words away. "Lots of people cry," she says.

"I don't," I say. "All of this is new."

NATURE HAS ITS SAY

AMBER WONG

Harmony, balance, rhythm. There you have it. That is what life is all about.

—George Pocock, leading designer and builder of racing shells

High above the Pocock Rowing Center dock, freeway traffic roars louder than usual, loud enough to pain my ears. I wince; at 6:15 in the morning, Seattle traffic, like the water, should be still. For the first time since March 8, 2020, I lean over and slip a sculling shell into the water, watch a ripple lap the dock. A gentle gust fans my black ponytail across my shoulders. What had been a simple joy a mere ten weeks ago now twists my gut into a gnarl of fear.

Before March 8, when winter chill still gripped the water, my rowing partner and I launched a double scull and relied on its broader girth to assure we'd never tip in. Most weekend mornings, dressed in matching black spandex tights and yellow hi-visibility rowing jackets, we'd skim past Portage Bay's house-boat dioramas—shoebox spaces starring bathrobed figures clutching mugs of coffee, aromas of bacon and pancakes oozing from their seams—and race east to the edge of Lake Washington, oars slashing through water in synchronous rhythm.

Panting hard we'd spin the boat, sip water, catch our breath in the view of snow-capped Cascade Mountains lit by the morning sun. On lucky days Mount Rainier would emerge, its crest glistening against the coral horizon.

On our return trip we'd watch for Union Bay's resident bald eagle pairs, their distinctive white heads and tail feathers stark even against a wintry gray sky. Once threatened with extinction, bald eagle populations slowly recovered under the protections of the 1973 Endangered Species Act, and we who lived through that peril marvel at the miracle of their return. A local birder has even named "our" eagles. We'd look for Eva and Albert, smug sentries of the wealthy Broadmoor neighborhood, as we passed the cottonwood at the northern tip of Foster Island. Talia and Russ kept their distance, preferring the mucky wetlands of the Union Bay Nature Reserve, while Monty and Marsha bickered loudly as they upgraded their nest at the mouth of the Montlake Cut. Any sighting was a thrill; a six-eagle day was a jackpot.

After every row we'd wipe down the boat, heft it onto its rack. "Coffee?" one of us might ask, mostly a formality. We'd stroll across the street to Le Fournil café, our rowing club's regular hangout. Sometimes we sat with others, sometimes we sat apart. Always we'd sip Americanos, split a breakfast baguette, recap our eagle sightings, and be back to our respective homes by 9.

But the speed and ferocity of the pandemic disrupted all routines, infused me with almost paralyzing fear. On March 11, days after my last row, news broke that the World Health Organization had declared the coronavirus outbreak a pandemic. Reaction was swift. Our governor announced the closure of Washington's schools. All after-school programs, including at our boathouse, shut down immediately. But late that night came news that gripped me by the throat: one of our adult rowers had been positively diagnosed with COVID-19. The entire boathouse would close indefinitely, all card keys inactivated. My fingertips went cold. *Who was it?* Was I talking to them just three days ago? I mentally retraced my steps. My pulse pounded with the unanswerable question: How risky is COVID-19 to me, a member of the over-60, "high-risk" population?

So in early June, after three months of frenzied hand sanitizing, mask wearing, and strategic racing through the supermarket every third week, when the boathouse announced a phased reopening, I went numb just thinking about it. Was rowing allowed under Washington's stay-at-home order? How would we avoid contaminating others, contaminating ourselves? Immediately my phone pinged. My rowing partner. Words tumbling, I felt her excitement, her caution, her ultimate plea. *Should we get out in singles next week? Maybe at sunrise to avoid people? New rules are: access to boat bays only, locker rooms off-limits. Only four people on a dock. Must reserve a boat and dock time online. Sanitize boats. Wear masks while on land.* And then, the clincher. *Eagles?*

So I'm standing here on the dock at 6:15 sharp, toes curling with cold, zipping up my hi-vis jacket and yanking gloves from the waistband of my spandex tights. My single scull dabs in the water as seagulls shriek overhead. Even though rowing conditions are excellent—51 degrees, no wind—I feel my heart pound, sense something sour deep in my gullet. Each spring the transition from a double scull to a single usually involves more mental preparation than this, and today six new safety procedures are clanging in my head. Stretching my shoulders to calm myself, I startle as a shadow darts behind me. I whirl around. Will that rower stay six feet away? Why is the traffic so loud? My ears pick up every tire squeal, every clomp from every pothole.

I grab my oars, slide onto my seat. Although I'm not Catholic, I feel an overwhelming urge to cross myself.

I hold my breath and launch.

Ten wobbly strokes later, 20 feet out in the middle of an empty channel, I finally remove my mask. I inhale deeply, exhale slowly. To the west rises the iconic silhouette of the Space Needle. With newly confident strokes I spin my boat toward the east, glance behind me, and set my course.

IN 1982, I went to see what is now a cult classic, Francis Ford Coppola's *Koyaanisqatsi: Life Out of Balance*. Rich in image, set to an ethereal soundtrack by Philip Glass, the mostly unscripted documentary film explores the tension between the natural and civilized worlds. The soundtrack is haunting, a recurrent chant reverberates even when it recedes. Mainly the film left me with the image of a frantic train station, film speeded up, people rushing toward what they thought was important, lost in their own universes. For days I pondered a new conundrum: *Where is the intersection, the right balance, between nature and civilization? For me? For the earth?*

Thirty-eight years and a pandemic later, I understand the world much differently. If the premise of *Koyaanisqatsi* was that life is out of balance, tilted irrevocably toward faster and faster engulfment of the natural world by the civilized, the eruption of the novel coronavirus sends the message that nature can fight back. Get its due. Have its say. And for me, a fan of science fiction and, I quietly admit, Marvel comics, the theme feels eerily familiar. An unimaginable catastrophe emerges. People deny its existence. It grows. Everyone ignores the experts. Politicians respond with hubris, confident that nature can be easily controlled. With inaction and chaotic messaging, the problem explodes, threatening all of civilization.

As the COVID-19 pandemic wreaks havoc across the globe, I feel I've slipped into that fantastical world, a world where, at least on screen, it all works out in the end. I paint the coronavirus a shadowed archvillain, a bloated purple menace, its maniacal cackle resonating around New York skyscrapers, above Ohio cornfields, through the Badlands, over the Cascade Mountains and across Lake Washington, echoing in the cavernous boat bays of my Seattle boathouse. The miasmic hulk reaches across a burning horizon, gloating at the world's panic, its helplessness, its despair. Teaming up with its cousin, the aptly named *Influenza horribilis*, together—at some remote arctic outpost—they plot the next wave of attacks, maliciously intoning, "Soon the world will be ours!" Impotent politicians wring their hands. In this cataclysmic clash between nature and civilization, how malevolent will the coronavirus be in leveraging its position? What sacrifice will it demand for civilization to be allowed to continue? Scenes of destruction fill the screen. A triumphant *Bwah-ha-ha* reverberates through ruined canyons and crushed cityscapes. All seems lost.

Only when the scene shifts to bespectacled scientists in white lab coats, urgently conferring among themselves, do I start to breathe easy.

Because lab coats speak to me. They say, "Science is Truth." Forty years ago I was a research engineer at Battelle-Northwest Laboratories, a specialist in the biological treatment of wastes. With my long black hair caught in a ponytail, goggles perched on my tiny nose, my lab coat—blue, not white—protected me from the burn of concentrated acids and the splash of bacterial sludge as I mixed chemical reagents and took samples from bench-scale biological reactors, trying to biodegrade a novel industrial wastewater. Success, in the world of waste treatment, relies on nurturing the growth of microbes that "eat" contaminants. Which microbes can metabolize this contaminant? What are their optimal pH and temperature conditions? I tweaked each condition, a couple of degrees here, a longer detention time there, to find the best option. Taming nature—or more accurately, working with nature—is like tending a fragile relationship where "balance of power" is a myth. It's a test of human accommodation, of respecting biological systems and their specific needs.

Though I'm not an epidemiologist, quashing the novel coronavirus seems to present similar challenges, only in reverse. Success lies in *preventing* the virus from thriving, so their task is to create hostile conditions, both outside the body and in. Outside's easier than inside. Viruses need hosts, so it's intuitive to keep people apart. Viruses sail between hosts in nose and mouth droplets, so it's also intuitive to add a mask barrier. By maintaining physical and spatial barriers between prospective hosts, fewer viruses glom onto a person. Wash them with soap, and they die.

Inside's the tougher battle. Rapid progress has been made, but the science isn't fully understood. Does the virus attack the young the same as the old? Do people with higher viral loads experience more severe symptoms? How is the virus mutating, and is it becoming more virulent? But there's hope. While effective drug treatments and preventative vaccines are not yet widely available, they do exist for similar coronaviruses. That's why I'm cautiously optimistic that we will find tools to live with, if not fully vanquish, this virus. I have faith in those white-lab-coated scientists.

I admit that my rosy confidence in science may be rooted in my childhood fascination with science fiction. I loved Isaac Asimov's entire robot series—Dr. Susan Calvin was such a badass!—and ultimately cheered for the habitually late protagonist in Harlan Ellison's "'Repent Harlequin!' Said the Ticktock Man." But the story that resounds most clearly in 2020 is Ray Bradbury's "A Sound of Thunder." Published in 1952, this short story combines time travel and dinosaurs, two of my favorite literary tropes. In the first known literary evocation of "the butterfly effect," Bradbury issues a harsh warning about human carelessness in messing with Mother Nature. The story's set far into the future. A big game hunter time-travels back to the Late Cretaceous period to bag a dinosaur. Although he's been warned repeatedly to stay on the floating path, precautions aren't foolproof; he accidentally steps off. When he returns to the future, he finds that the social and political system he left has been totally upended, his worst fears realized. Even the rules of spelling have been corrupted. In the mud of his boots, he finds a crushed butterfly. The Butterfly Effect, the premise of chaos theory that a seemingly inconsequential change can have a catastrophic outcome, seems to have come into play this year. As a child I understood this story to be fiction. Now I wonder.

BEFORE THE PANDEMIC, rowing teams hoisted eight-person boats on their shoulders and marched in steady rhythm toward the dock while nimble rowers with single sculls atop their heads stepped out of the way. Boats are long, riggers are wide, so it seems a miracle that in the mad scramble to get boats on the water there were so few collisions in the boathouse, so few arguments about who got to go first.

As I pace my warm-up under the shadow of the University Bridge, I'm somehow reminded of that train station film clip from *Koyaanisqatsi*. But now I interpret the scene differently. Instead of focusing on the frantic commuter bustle, I slow the clip to its real-life speed. Now I'm watching a river of people flowing smoothly, weaving among each other along individual paths, gliding in a controlled rhythm. There's no cog out of sync, no collision, no giant pileup. The system works because everyone knows what they're supposed to do. They're like rowers. We've learned to keep aware of our bodies, and our outsized equipment, in space. It's a delicate dance, a balance between individual desires to get on the water quickly and respect for the rowing community's collective harmony. Our gangly equipment does its part by enforcing social distancing. All this time I'd never known it would become our pandemic response writ small.

I peek over my shoulder and angle my single scull into the calm of Portage Bay. On the straightaway I press hard, streaming past the houseboats and their backlit inhabitants on my way to the edge of Lake Washington. My oars grip the water with increasing force. My muscles lengthen. I feel the wind at my back, taste the air fresh from the rain. Blisters are starting to form on my hands. And still, I hope for eagles.

WHY I PLACED MINIMALISM ON THE SHELF DURING THE PANDEMIC

AUTUMN PURDY

In the days before the COVID-19 virus became a part of our vernacular, before the world and our lives changed overnight, I identified as a minimalist. I read every book written on simplicity, bought tickets to The Minimalists' *Less Is Now Tour*, and decluttered until sparks flew and I was on fire as a model of modest living. I kept a sparse pantry, pristine refrigerator, organized closets, and streamlined shelves. Rarely did I plan beyond a month in advance. I seldom bought items in bulk. I pared down from roof to basement, let go of excess household goods and attire, even donated books.

My existing pandemic lifestyle is anything but organized and refined. Last March, as my family and I remained sheltered at home, I started to lose my resolve for minimalism. Instead of discarding more, I began adding back complex layers to my inner and outer world. In the name of COVID-19, I grew defiant and leery of keeping too little in a time of crisis. So, I abandoned my oversimplified self—placed her way up high on a shelf where she could be admired, but not easily accessed—and gave in to the ways of my former, maximalist persona, freeing her from the mantelpiece of the past.

Now, my bookshelves are overflowing again with public library drive-thru reserves and a vast selection curated from online purchases and "Little Free Library" finds. At present, my basement pantry is stockpiled with canned, bottled, boxed, and bagged goods, a multiplying grouping of hand soap refills, and any brand disinfectant cleaner I find. Tucked away in the back corner of the master bedroom closet, I store an overflowing mound of Kotex, size 4T training pants, and baby wipes. Critical supplies—thermometer, acetaminophen and ibuprofen, honey lozenges, Vitamin C drops, tissues, masks, gloves, Lysol, antibacterial gel, and bottled water—are within reach in a basket atop my dresser. A bin of outgrown children's clothing hides in basement storage because I felt no urgency to consign them. A donation bag sits in limbo against the wall. For the first time, I bought my children's school supplies online and postponed the sorting and labeling while I eagerly awaited the final verdict on the academic year ahead.

Before the pandemic, I resisted veering from my weekly, monthly, or seasonal cleaning schedules. These days, I tidy the house at will, on a whim, if at all—except for the bathrooms, kitchen counters and appliances, and all door handles and light switches—those surfaces are scrubbed daily with a fierce determination to eradicate the invisible germs of a lingering, life-threatening residue carried in from the outside. Though I still tackle laundry with regularity, I now own a three-pound bag of Charlie's Soap to last my family through the next 300 washes.

Affixed to the refrigerator door is the whiteboard weekly dinner menu I haven't erased nor updated since, perhaps, April 2020. I no longer recall the exact date when my family and I dined on "lamb, roasted asparagus, and redskin potatoes." Yet, I know it was a Sunday, and I planned leftovers for the next day because my slanted scrawl in black Expo marker offers lasting proof. Now, I humbly allow others to grocery shop for me and I am grateful for the service. I've not opened my favorite cookbooks in a year, preferring lately to prepare uncomplicated meals by heart. Gone are the days spent rushing from store to store in search of obscure ingredients for an elaborate dinner. Lately, I worry less about the feast itself and more about how the food I cook fills our bellies with healthy doses of comfort at a time when we could all use an ounce or two more of tender care. I'm surrendering to minimizing in the kitchen and maximizing time well-spent with my husband and kids around the dinner table.

Despite the necessary resurgence of excessive living that I've allowed during 2020, I haven't forgotten how the edicts of minimalism saved me during a bleak period in my life, a stretch when I was completely debilitated by a mix of tragedy and change that transpired in rapid succession: suffering my sixth miscarriage, grappling with my mom's cancer diagnosis, taking extra precautions during a subsequent high-risk pregnancy further complicated by placenta previa, managing the challenges of one child's declining mental health and another's newly diagnosed life-threatening food allergies, and to cap it all off, an unexpected, extra-long recovery after my third caesarean. I was overwhelmed, my days were a chaotic mess, we were buried under a mound of stuff, and I was longing for peace. The serenity I was seeking was initially gleaned by paring down my family's calendar and maintaining an organized home.

It took me years to reap the benefits of living a minimalist lifestyle, to realize what stretched the boundaries of my comfort zone, learn how to loosen the reins of want over true need, and witness the full effects of how simplifying my environment helped cleanse me from within. Every ounce of sweat, bag packed, item sold, and piece of debris swept away was worth the effort. As I donated and discarded more and released the vice grip of material things, I suddenly discovered greater peace of mind and fullness of heart. Plus, there was room to breathe, relax, and enjoy the space my family and I call home.

What my newfound, reformed lifestyle *did not* prepare me for was how to live through a pandemic with its ensuing shutdowns, virtual schooling, halted social interaction and enhanced full-family time, nor how to deal with the host of other emotional stressors and valid fears 2020 ushered in with a vengeance.

The tenacity I adhered to for tidiness and sparseness started to dwindle as one season bled into the other, and then another, and yet another. As I started to pull away from the control of daily order toward more pressing, imperative duties, a new stirring began to arise within me in the form of questions: What constitutes adequate masking? Am I making safe decisions regarding the validity of running an errand once deemed harmless and necessary? Are my children washing their hands long enough? When will it ever be safe to go to the grocery store, the post office, the dentist? How long will they/I have to participate in virtual schooling? Are my kids learning anything? How long will we be sheltering in place? Will we ever not need technology to communicate intimately with our loved ones? How can I ensure all facets of my family members' lives are met with love and compassion? How are their hearts, minds, bodies, and spirits faring through the long-suffering season of shutdowns and letdowns? How can I maintain some semblance of my former self, hold on to hope, survive the devastation? Will this pandemic make us or break us?

Recently, my daughter and I entered Target for the second time together since the shutdown last year. Masks on and shopping list in hand, we needed only a handheld basket to collect our necessities. During our hyper-focused search, we discovered two shelves filled with the holy grail of 2020: disinfectant wipes. I swear I broke out in tears in the middle of aisle B3, my gawking expression suggesting I had perhaps struck gold, as cleaning wipes clearly *are* gold in these unwieldy times. Elatedly, I placed one, allotted tub in my red basket and skipped down to aisle CL13 for face wash.

After returning home from the shopping trip, I presented the disinfectant wipes to my husband like it was his newborn child. He validated my tears of joy and appreciated the lucky find, understanding that this item symbolized comfort and peace. He may have even high-fived me on the way to the basement—my shrine to the precious jewels mined out of a pandemic—to find a premiere spot for this coveted treasure, the rarest of COVID-19 gems.

The prudent me isn't completely buried under the necessary excess. Certainly, minimalism maintains its merit. One day soon, I hope I can dust off the minimalist me, bring her down from high up on the shelf, and back to solid ground where she truly belongs. For the time being, I'm safe-keeping my affinity for simple living like a precious knick-knack from a bygone era on a dusty shelf while ensuring my family has what we need without crossing over the line to hoarding.

The minimalism I once sought was a deliberate act of paring down overabundance, and eschewing excess; it proved to be a soul-searching practice that taught me how to let go. My best guess is years will pass before pandemic lessons are revealed to me, for better or for worse. For now, during this unpredictable era, I'm choosing to remain confident in one certainty I've managed to uncover despite the newly acquired clutter: stockpile all that's worth holding on to—nothing more, nothing less.

STAGE MOTHER

GRETCHEN M. MICHELFELD

"You need to work on your soliloquy before dinner and don't forget you have your Zoom vocal recital this weekend and your piano teacher wants you to learn 'I Dreamed a Dream' by Wednesday!"

If you had told me 12 years ago that the sweet little baby in my arms would one day hear these words come out of my mouth, I'd have spat on the ground three times and run screaming.

During the two decades I pursued a New York City theatre career, I encountered countless child actors and cringed at their often controlling, single-minded stage parents. I'll never forget the little boy in the big, starry Christmas musical I assistant-directed, who was more professional than half the adults in the show, but who whispered to me through tears one day, "I wanted to sign up for softball, but I'm not allowed because I haven't landed a commercial yet." I could never be a stage mother! Yet here I am sounding like Mama Rose.

My pre-pandemic pre-teen played basketball and loved his bike. He got good grades, he liked reading and chess. But he was also a dramarama. A theatre nerd. Just like his mom. Sigh. My

husband and I have tried to set boundaries and realistic expectations. No headshots. No agents. We have said "Yes" to
student films and community theatre, but we've managed to
avoid getting sucked into the child-actor world, which is no
small feat in New York City. Rather than fantasies of stardom,
we have encouraged him to focus on friendships and cama-
raderie with other kids who love to sing and dance. For years I
spent my Sundays writing at the café around the corner from
the little children's theatre where he took class. Then I'd read in
the lounge of the music studio next door during his singing
lesson. We'd often have lunch with other Sunday-theatre-class
families. It was all very sociable and cozy. But when the
pandemic hit and the world shut down, there was no more of
any of that.

As his basketball season was cancelled and school went
remote, my kid's frustration and fear distracted him. He stopped
reading. He said he hated school.

The children's theatre closed. The staff continued to teach
remotely, and he tried it for a while, but it wasn't the same. Or
maybe he was just outgrowing it. He certainly outgrew his bike,
and though we planned to buy him a new one for his birthday,
that was still a few months away.

His days became nothing more than going through the
motions—a fuzzy haze of YouTube videos and grumpy online
gaming with his equally frustrated friends. I made us go for
walks. I made us play board games. I made healthy meals. But
still, he languished. I knew we needed a big juicy project to sink
our teeth into. But nothing inspired him.

And then one day at dinner, he declared, "I want to audition for Frank Sinatra."

Frank Sinatra School of the Arts is a conservatory-style
performing arts high school in Astoria, Queens. It may not boast
the kinds of starry alums that Manhattan's LaGuardia High

School does, but it gives the world-renowned "Fame" school a run for its money.

Admissions are by audition only. Two monologues and a song.

We were never going to be the pandemic-baking, learn-a-new-language, Shakespeare-wrote-*King-Lear*-during-the-plague kind of family. But two monologues and a song? Here was our big juicy project.

We had already decided to continue his singing lessons online, and the one-on-one lesson format actually worked well over Zoom. His teacher suggested a keyboard iPad app so he could find his pitch and pluck out songs as he practiced, but when we found a second-hand Casio Privia for $100, my son asked for piano lessons. Terrific! The more time spent on music lessons, the less time wasted lying on his bed streaming videos about extreme bacon recipes and epic sports fails.

For Christmas, we bought him some monologue books and I called upon a dear childhood friend, a veteran Broadway and Regional actor who runs a theatre company in Houston and teaches classes. Did he teach online? Yes. Suddenly we had a monologue coach and the kid was learning a soliloquy from *Henry IV, Part 1*.

My son performed in an online singing recital. He was invited to participate in a social justice-oriented theatre project, with kids from all over New York meeting online to write and rehearse. A few weeks ago, he downloaded a workout app and added nightly burpees and pushups to his singing, piano, and acting routine.

And now I marvel at this disciplined, focused, 12-year-old with whom I live. This is my son. He wants to audition for a performing arts high school. And, oh dear, I'm starting to sound like some of those parents of the show business kids I worked with years ago. Because my boy isn't *always* disciplined and, although we are fortunate to be able to afford his lessons, we are throwing money away if he doesn't take them seriously. When I hear myself reminding him to learn his lines or do his warm-ups, I tell myself that I am not that mom who told her kid he had to land a commercial before she'd let him play sports. I try to remember that this is what he has right now and he needs to make the most of it. He can't go to school, or parties, or basketball games. He can't visit his grandparents or go to a movie. But he has this dream and this newfound work ethic.

For now, I guess that means I'm a stage mother.

SHOULD I OWN THIS? Should I take a second look at the stage parents I've known? Maybe one of those moms realized her boy wasn't great at sports, didn't love schoolwork, was going through an awkward transition into pre-pubescence, and was having trouble with his friends. If I'm honest with myself, maybe that was me even *before* the pandemic.

Because I must admit he's happier singing Sondheim than shooting hoops. Just as he began despairing that his athletic, sports-crazy childhood friends were leaving him behind, his fellow pre-teen thespians started telling him he was awesome, which certainly warms a mother's heart.

The same heart that was broken over and over again in the pursuit of her own theatrical career.

And there's the rub. I fear the vicarious thrills. I shun them.

OVER THE PAST 12 MONTHS, I have done much reminiscing. When one spends one's day behind a mask, one tends to look within, examine personal history, remember each triumph and rejection with renewed clarity. Yes, I desperately wanted to succeed in theatre. Yes, I feel left behind by all of my friends who are still in the game. But how much of my struggle was simply a struggle to make my *own* mother happy, give her something to brag about, give her attention and applause through me?

I keep telling myself that this is his life. He does not need to succeed in theatre to make up for my past disappointments. My job is to raise him to be a good, healthy, happy young man. His job is to find something he cares about enough to work hard at, right?

As I write this, I hear him in the next room singing "Getting Tall" from *Nine,* and his voice cracks. I am aware of the irony. Every time I hear him practice "Not While I'm Around" from *Sweeney Todd,* I feel just like Toby, the character he's playing. I want to protect him from the demons who will charm him with a smile and the tease of success on the Great White Way. But then I remember that he's managed to find some beauty in this horrible year. He's captured a bit of joy. Sometimes his humanity takes my breath away.

Maybe it's OK to be a stage mother. Maybe we're doing just fine.

WE WERE LUCKY

JENNY MOORE

When the pandemic began, my son was two. He attended a small day care in a neighbor's home and, miraculously, it stayed open. Inadvertently, we formed a quasi-pod with the other day care families. As the weeks stretched into months, everyone stayed healthy. Most of us kept our jobs. We were lucky.

My mother called my son "the miracle baby." Conceived after years of IVF as my husband and I were on the verge of giving up, he arrived in 2017 healthy and happy. Birth wasn't his only miracle. While I was in labor, my mother received a diagnosis of a rare, hard-to-treat lymphoma. The doctor recommended chemotherapy as soon as possible, but my mother delayed for a few weeks so she could meet her new grandson on the East Coast. When she began to feel better, I wondered if she was on a short-lived grandma high. But after she returned to her home in the Southwest, another scan showed the cancer was in spontaneous remission. The doctors were nonplussed. It was rare without treatment, they said. Lucky.

When the pandemic began, I was 46. For days, then weeks that spring, I waited for the virus to hit my household. We knew so little, only that it was bad and it was everywhere. At night the darkest possibilities crept in. Any of our loved ones could get sick and die on a ventilator, so alone. My husband and I could get sick simultaneously. Expose someone else. Lose our jobs. If we were both hospitalized, who would care for our son? I imagined him orphaned at two, raised by strangers in a post-COVID world where no one he knew survived and the life we imagined for him had blown apart. During the days while my son was at day care and I was supposed to be working, I struggled to focus. I went outside and dug up the bamboo that spread across our yard. As I sank a spade beneath the invasive roots, I thought, desperately, *Not here. Not today.*

When the pandemic began, my mother was 74. In mid-March she was traveling, visiting my brother and one set of oncologists in California. She flew back to her home in the desert after much of the country was shut down. She was already used to wearing a mask. The previous year she had finally gotten chemo when the cancer returned, and once again it was in remission. Her hair had grown back and her energy was good. She took excellent care of herself, better than anyone I knew. Though she felt occasional symptoms, signs of rebellion within her body, she stayed healthy. There it is again: lucky.

Time froze in some ways, the days crawling by in seclusion and sameness with no hope of change. The grim news bore down on everything. Some people were lucky and some people terribly not so. In other ways, time pushed us forward. My son was toilet training and outgrowing day care. We spoke a new language: contact tracing and pods, elbow bumps and doomscrolling. We scrambled to find elastic strips for masks, then ended up buying shitty, first-generation ones online. My mother was supposed to visit in April for her birthday. We canceled the trip, of course. Spring stepped aside for summer.

EVERY DAY I thought about the precarious balance of our situation. One small shift, one molecule or upward tick in numbers, one cough or modified cell, would bring everything crashing down. Our day care situation seemed tenuous, though it also seemed to be holding. The preschool we had chosen was preparing to open in the fall with stringent precautions. We felt we could tolerate the greater risk of exposure, but depending on school to stay safely open seemed naïve. Some of my work is impossible to do with a child present. *Buckle up,* I kept thinking.

Always, in the back of my mind, I knew my mother was going to need me. The cancer was not gone, just receded. She lived alone. It was when, not if. I refused to consider the possibility that I wouldn't be able to get to her safely. When she talked about how lonely she was, how it drove her crazy to just sit at home so far from her family, I felt guilty we couldn't visit her. But a three-day drive with a toddler was out of the question, and my son on an airplane full of germs would be a nightmare. He had never worn a mask. He licked furniture for fun. I daydreamed about her moving in with us so that I could care for both my mother and my son without feeling torn.

After agonized deliberations, my mother decided to fly east for my son's third birthday. When she arrived she quarantined, and came to stay with us two weeks later. We had long daily hugs. My son jumped into her bed each morning. She was in heaven. We went on walks and cooked and did crossword puzzles and talked about nothing and everything. She seemed to be well, though she tired easily, and a few times when I asked how she felt she paused, then made a face and shrugged.

She flew home the day before preschool started. When I picked up my son at the end of the first day he was still wearing his mask, and we were off. Preschool allowed his world to open up rather than close down. After two weeks of isolating at home, my mother was COVID-free after the trip. Lucky, lucky, lucky.

In September she felt more signs that the cancer was back, and soon the familiar cycle began: appointments, scans and biopsies, consultations, treatment. At one point she told me, with resignation, "The cancer center is my pod."

One evening at the end of the month, my son got a low fever, followed by a runny nose. It took ten days to get his test result (negative) while we waited to feel our own symptoms or hear about an outbreak at school or work.

It was difficult to imagine visiting my mother, even if I went alone. Preschool and work meant we were always potentially exposed. I could get the virus from the airplane and transmit it to her. Once I flew home, my son would not be able to return to school until we had isolated for two weeks, and after taking time off for the visit, additional time away from work would be difficult. I didn't want to risk getting her sick or getting sick myself. I didn't want to leave my son. It was easier to operate as though the hiatus from life was temporary, that soon we would regain everything we had lost. My mom kept being okay, bouncing back, a little slower each time. I pushed away my unease—I'd gotten used to it—and we talked every day, as we had for years before the pandemic.

SHE FOUND the desert after divorcing. She embraced it fully, learning the culture and soaking up the landscape and making strong friendships. But she had no family nearby, and it was hard for us to get to her. I was almost 2,000 miles away, my brother 1,000. Her three siblings were also far away, and none were vaccinated.

As the weather turned colder her symptoms flared, and while she waited for treatment she had radiation to treat tumors. Zap here, zap there. There was a clinical trial beginning the week of Thanksgiving. Friends brought her groceries and drove her to appointments. My brother and I monitored from our respective coasts.

Within a week of starting the trial, her symptoms were much worse than the drug's expected side effects. Within a week, my brother got in his car and drove to see her. Within a week, the doctors removed her from the trial and scheduled another treatment. But she couldn't begin that medication until after the trial drug cleared her system. I thought of it as a race, and cancer was pulling ahead.

In mid-December she was hospitalized, and there she improved. A doctor gently but firmly initiated a sobering conversation about the end of her life. The fact of her death, which had been sitting far ahead of us, was suddenly close. Maybe in a few months, a year perhaps. But cancer was going to win. Panic struck me hard. My mom was leaving. I didn't know how to bear it. That night, she and I had a video call that lasted two hours. We talked and checked in and fought back tears and just were together.

I bought a plane ticket, face shields. Packed extra wipes and tried not to breathe hard. I anticipated a new phase where I would make multiple trips over the months to come and we'd be super careful and I'd figure out a rhythm with my husband and son. I didn't see a choice.

When I arrived at her house, she did not stand up to greet me. Her discomfort—pain—was constant. Her body had changed, torso and legs swollen, shoulders and arms gaunt. That night I made her dinner and she ate three bites and we opened Christmas presents and watched the first episode of "Bridgerton." She was weaker the next day, and in the evening we went to the hospital. Two days later I was able to be with her when she died. I knew, especially in a pandemic, that I was lucky for that.

IT IS SPRING AGAIN, and my son is still in school. I spend my time working, or managing my mother's affairs. I try to make space for the loss.

I tell myself that I'm lucky. It wasn't COVID that killed her. I was able to fly to see her and I did not have to sit helpless thousands of miles away while she died alone. I hugged her—the threat of COVID didn't matter anymore. I helped her stand up. I was there when her spirit left her body, when the sun streaming through the window shone on her, and I knew that she—the life force that gave me life—was gone.

This is what passes for luck now. I try to be grateful for the things I know could be worse. We are in a pandemic and staggering numbers of people are dead, but my son still has his parents. My mom had to die from cancer, but she had time in remission, and treatment gave us three more years with her. Since the day my son was born, I've known I was going to lose my mother while he was young, but I finally have a child after years of trying. She's gone, but I was by her side when she left.

My tendency to temper the losses is an attempt at self-preservation. They are too big if I look at them directly. Also, I still prefer gratitude to doomscrolling.

Grief makes its own precarious balance. We were lucky, but my heart is still broken in a new place. COVID stole days with my mother that can never be restored. For months she had to be alone and wait for the cancer to come for her. My guilt turns to anger, which turns to sorrow. If I hadn't been afraid of the virus and struggling to balance everything else, if I'd known we were out of time, I would have been on the first flight to the desert and hugged her and rubbed her feet and leaned my head on her shoulder or pressed her head to mine while sitting side by side on the couch, and I would have told her in much more detail just how much I loved her, and every word would have been sweeter because we have seen each other through a lot and our last decade was our best decade together.

She knew my world, and I knew hers, and when my son thinks I hung the moon I think of my mother and how she once was everything to me that I now am to him. I keep moving forward and keep functioning and I love my family and I miss her. Vaccinated, I wear my mask and wait for the world to emerge from isolation. Sometimes I cry, but always, inside, I feel dystopian: This pandemic and my mother's absence, forever entwined, have blasted a hole through me. I tell myself that within that desiccated landscape any drop of water is good fortune, a sign of life.

LOCKDOWN

ELLYN GELMAN

I wake to unfamiliar silence. The urgent energy of pedestrians and traffic that normally mark my days has been muted. An ambulance screams up Tenth Avenue and leaves a quiet in its wake that begs to be held. The carriage horses stabled a block away no longer clip-clop their way toward Central Park. The joy of children as they line up for school at PS 111 is lost to stay-at-home orders. A city never meant for silence has lost its voice. The elevator doors rarely ding, and it feels as though I'm living alone on the entire 12th floor. For the first time since I moved to 52nd Street and 10th Avenue 18 months ago, I can hear the endless chatter of sparrows.

I rearrange my pillow and consider staying in bed. Nina startles me when she jumps up and stares me down with her intense green eyes. I consider myself a dog person, but I agreed to provide temporary shelter for my niece's 13-pound gray cat. Nina arrived yesterday in the pouring rain.

My niece pulled up in front of my building and we off-loaded Nina's cat supplies onto a luggage cart. The apartment she had planned to rent is unavailable because the elderly woman who occupies the apartment is unable to move to assisted living due to COVID-19 restrictions. We are all business as she hands me her beloved cat in a black carrier. Our glasses steam up under our face masks. We don't hug, and she doesn't come up for a chat and a cup of tea. As I wheel past the concierge, Nina's meows grow to wails. "It's only temporary," I say to the young man behind the desk as I rush toward the elevators. If he reports me to the leasing office, my rent will increase 50 dollars a month.

I get out of bed and pour kibble into Nina's bowl. I make a cup of coffee and open the blinds in my living room. "Good morning, New York City," I say as I've said every day since I moved here. Some days I whisper in awe and some days I shout with joy, but I never miss saying good morning to the city because it reminds me that I had the guts to follow my dream.

In order to do so, I had to pull the plug on a 35-year marriage lingering on life-support. When my husband said, "I am *never* moving to the city," he made it clear that my vision of the future ran parallel to his with no hope of merging. A week later, I leased an apartment. With my American Express card, I purchased a bed, a few pieces of furniture, a table to write at, and a set of cheap white dishes. I felt light, ready to write, find a job, and absorb all that Manhattan had to offer.

Today the city is shrouded in gray and the top floors of the Empire State Building to my right and the Central Park Tower to my left, disappear into the low ceiling.

"Hey, Google, what is the date today?" I say.

"Today is Monday, March 30th," my home mini reports.

There is no need to change. My sleeping clothes—soft black leggings and a t-shirt—have become my day clothes. Despite my dread, I turn on the news and learn that there are over 56,000 cases of COVID-19 citywide. 914 people have died. I find it hard to wrap my head around the fact that almost a thousand people, alive and well a month ago, are dead. That is the same number of temporary hospital beds FEMA has set up in the Javits Center. One thousand is the entire audience at a showing of *Dear Evan Hanson* at the Music Box Theater. 138 people, close to the same number of people who live in my apartment building, died overnight. The intensive care units are overwhelmed and there's a shortage of oxygen tanks.

Governor Cuomo repeats that the worst is yet to come. There is no mask mandate although many are wearing them. Dr. Fauci said on *60 Minutes* that there is no reason to be walking around with a mask. He said that masks may block some droplets, but they do not provide the level of protection people think they do. I don't know what to believe, but I know a mask can't hurt. The mask I purchased on Etsy is made of a polyester and lycra blend and smells like a wet bathing suit when I breathe into it. I sent the same masks to my 28-year-old son and his fiancée who live on West 57th Street, my 23-year-old daughter who lives in Philadelphia, and her twin brother in Salt Lake City.

The naval hospital ship, the USNS *Comfort* with its 750 beds, is scheduled to dock on the Hudson River today. I watch television footage as the ship, flanked by the Coast Guard, makes its way under the Verrazano-Narrows Bridge and passes the Statue of Liberty. All my windows face east, so I head out of my apartment to watch it dock from the west-facing window in the hallway by the elevators. The sight of the hospital ship painted white and marked with multiple red crosses docking next to the USS *Intrepid* gives me goosebumps. Perhaps it is relief that help from outside the city has arrived or perhaps it is the fact that I am bearing witness to what I pray is a once-in-a-lifetime experience.

Another ambulance blares its way up 10th Avenue as I re-enter my apartment and reminds me that I am a non-essential worker. I have been furloughed from my part-time job as an usher at an Off-Broadway theater, the workshop where I teach a writing class is between terms, and the church uptown where I volunteer in a homework help program has been shuttered. My only job now is to protect others by my own confinement. And Nina.

I sit at my small table and open my laptop. Nina settles on the other chair and falls asleep. From where I sit, I can see all 624 square feet of my apartment, but it feels as if it is slowly shrinking without my usual escapes to museums, matinees, book readings, and art classes. I came here to immerse myself in the rhythms of the city, but this is not the New York I signed up for. I picture my husband gloating in our house in the suburbs. Nina lifts her head when I snort. I scratch her head, "I would rather live here in a lockdown than return to my old life," I tell her. Nina stretches, licks a front paw, and falls back to sleep.

I make another cup of coffee and throw in a load of laundry before I return to the blank screen. I Google "New York City carriage horses" and discover that most of them have been transferred to Amish farms out of state. I check that off my worry list, but there are more. They rise to the surface like tiny bubbles just before water boils. This past year has confirmed what I have to admit I already knew: There is not much interest in hiring a woman knocking at the door to 60 with a major gap in her career while she raised her children. The courts have shut down and divorce proceedings halted. My life is loaded with questions and my mind works overtime. When will I see my mother, my children, my friends? How is eight-year-old Daisy doing without my homework help? When the divorce is finally settled, will I be able to afford to stay in New York? Where will I go if I have to leave? None of my questions have answers.

I shut my laptop and curl up on the couch. Nina settles in against my belly and purrs like it's her job. I turn on the television and lose myself in Netflix.

Five hours later, my mother's face lights up my cell phone for what she refers to as her daily proof of life call. "How's it going there?" she asks.

"Pretty bleak."

"Well, at least you have a governor who cares."

"Are you outside?"

"Yes, feeding apples to the horses," she says. "Noah, don't grab."

I laugh and wonder how long it will take her to teach my sister's mini-horse proper manners. Brenda is a year younger than I am and lives on a small ranch with two horses, a mini-horse and four dogs, down in Lake County, Florida. All are rescues. Two weeks earlier, Brenda also rescued our 81-year-old mother from her assisted living facility where some staff members and a resident have already tested positive for COVID-19.

"That navy hospital ship arrived today. I'll text you the picture I took," I say.

She tells me that Brenda has installed a railing so she can get in and out of the pool, I tell her that I'm already attached to Nina, and we say goodbye.

I don my mask, take the elevator to the lobby where strips of blue painter's tape mark off the floor in six-foot sections. All the orange and chartreuse furniture has been removed to discourage socializing.

Once outside, I head west to see the hospital ship up close. The sun has burnt off the day's gloom and it feels good on my face. I am disappointed when I arrive to find that tarps have been latched to the chain-link fences to block the view. Members of the NYPD mill around in pairs. "Keep moving," they say to those who attempt to take photos in between the gaps. I walk uptown along the river in Riverside Park. Canadian geese feast on new shoots of grass. Fresh mulch fills the air with a musky promise, and I imagine the daffodils and tulips preparing themselves below ground. I walk off the path across the grass to strum the curtain of bright green buds on a weeping willow tree. Spring is unfazed by the pervasive uncertainty of this pandemic. Summer will soon follow, and this comforts me. I realize all I can do is what I can do today.

I arrive home shortly before seven and collect my wooden spoon and frying pan. Nina figure eights her body between my legs as I slide open the living room window and bang my pan along with thousands of other New Yorkers in what will become a daily ritual of appreciation for health care workers on the front line. It is a cacophony of whistles, clapping, banging, honking, and cheering. It is human connection, a new normal that will mark time in the dark days to come.

A YEAR IN THE LIFE OF A BLACK DIGITAL STRATEGIST

LESLIE MAC

While my work as an Organizer and Digital Strategist has always been urgent, this year brought a new sense of clarity to everything I do and reframed my place in the movement for Black Liberation.

I started 2020 on the presidential campaign trail as Digital Organizer for Black Womxn For, a project focused on creating intentional meeting spaces for Black women and gender non-conforming community leaders around the election, and as a surrogate for the Elizabeth Warren campaign. This work kept me on the road a lot, from Boston to Atlanta, Cedar Rapids, Iowa to Charleston, South Carolina, where I found myself as we all started understanding the seriousness of the COVID-19 pandemic.

I literally went from hosting campaign events on Super Tuesday Eve directly into lockdown back home in Charlotte. It was whiplash, and as a Digital Strategist, I was immediately aware that my skills were in need all around me. Grassroots organizers and organizations were forced to rethink all their remaining plans for the year. My first project along with The South was "Landing Digital," a combination digital organizing training and coaching program designed to skill up organizers and help them bridge the gap between how they were used to reaching their communities in person and utilizing online techniques.

As it became clear that the pandemic was going to last well into the summer, voter outreach organizations found themselves in the difficult position of attempting to maximize voter turnout while not having their usual in-person events, conventions, and gatherings. My calendar was soon full, producing virtual events and reworking voter engagement campaigns to heavily include digital outreach and more.

And then on May 25, George Floyd was murdered by Minneapolis police, on camera, in broad daylight. The news came to me directly from local organizers whom I have known, loved, and supported for years. As they were springing into action on the ground, national organizers quickly connected and started our collective work to support them via narrative clarification, amplifying local needs, getting the word out about which organizations to support, and centering the mental health and well-being of Black people everywhere.

We were all sadly used to these actions, but also quickly realized that this moment felt different than the many incidents of Black death at the hands of police we had dealt with in the past. The footage of Derek Chauvin murdering George Floyd as people pleaded with him to stop, coupled with months of a failed government response to the COVID-19 pandemic, meant our movement, The Movement for Black Lives, was reaching more people than ever and that more people were ready to actually *hear* what we have been screaming since the murder of Trayvon Martin: the simple truth that Black Lives Matter.

As we supported our folks in the Twin Cities, we also had to look ahead to the upcoming general election, knowing that turnout would be critical and that disinformation was targeting our communities. Many of us set our sights on making it safe and joyful for Black people to vote in November. As state after state attempted to make voting harder, even in the midst of COVID-19 ravaging Black, Brown, and Indigenous communities, a collective formed to protect our right to vote. This coalition, The Frontline, a joint endeavor of the Working Families Party, The Movement for Black Lives, United We Dream, and Rising Majority had the goal of mobilizing a fraction of the millions of people who took to the streets over the summer to ensure our communities had what they needed to vote safely by Election Day.

I signed on as Communications Director for The Frontline, and we worked hard all the way through the January 2021 Georgia Senate runoff election to deliver the possibility of change to Washington, DC. Our efforts, while successful, were swiftly met with over 400+ proposed bills in 40 states meant to suppress the vote. The tactics we used in the 2020 general election—providing water, PPE supplies, snacks, and information to voters—are direct targets of these new bills, and it is hard to put into words what it felt like to see our non-partisan work villainized so quickly.

The whiplash of hearing "Thank Black women" to these direct attacks on our organizing efforts is not without precedence, but they are still painful to deal with. For those of us fighting for true liberation, a new administration in the White House only meant a new set of opponents to our radical work. And as we were hurtling towards losing more than 500,000 Americans from COVID-19, unrelenting police brutality against protesters nationwide, and a Democratic party eager to return to a "normal" that was unable to care for and protect the most vulnerable people in our country, I found myself questioning all of my work. How could I best serve my community, while protecting myself, honoring my mental health, and being frank, allowing myself to rest after going non-stop for months and months?

This questioning led to a realignment of my work, a more proactive approach to my organizing, and being more honest with those around me about how I was doing and what I needed to keep doing the work I am called to do. Over the last year, I have traveled to Louisville, Kentucky multiple times to support local organizers doing deeply radical work in the wake of the murder of Breonna Taylor. I held online trainings for communications staff at organizations around the country and a few weeks ago helped launch #KeepIt100, a new coalition campaign from The Frontline, New Georgia Project, Fair Fight, Black Voters Matter, The Movement for Black Lives Electoral Justice Project, and the NAACP. Our work for freedom and justice never ends, but 2020 taught me that exhausting myself and allowing those around me to be pushed beyond their physical and emotional limits serves no one.

When people ask me what 2020 taught me, the list of lessons is long. I learned how talented our movement is, how committed Black people are to our own healing and freedom. I learned that "normal" is no longer enough, that we won't allow a complacent return to "business as usual," that our long fight for Black and collective liberation requires imaginative action. I learned that you can't legislate freedom. I learned that rest must be built into our work. I learned how easily white people will treat our fight as a fad and how little it takes for them to walk away from their commitments to our movements. I learned that we will be portrayed as villains by our opponents no matter what we do, so it's time to shed our fear and do what is needed to get free.

But above all, I learned that we must allow those on the frontline of the multi-racial movements against racism, homophobia, transphobia, ableism, and poverty to *rest*, to rejuvenate, and to fortify ourselves for the fights before us. If you know an organizer in your community, do all you can to materially support them to take time off. Ensure they have jobs that pay them well, make sure they are able to afford quality healthcare, childcare, access to healthy food, and mental health support in times of crisis and every day—this work is equally taxing on our bodies and minds. Directly supporting organizers is the best way to ensure a better tomorrow for us all.

CHRYSALIS SPRING

SHANNON CONNOR WINWARD

Last Christmas, Santa gave our bug-loving five-year-old a send-away for a live butterfly kit. In that gray, pre-COVID winter, it was a stocking-stuffer promise that seasons change, and that we were in for brighter days.

In early March 2020, as the shadow of a pandemic was mounting over the horizon, I flew home to Delaware from Los Angeles after my third unsuccessful spinal operation in seven months. Airport security in Philadelphia made me peel off my plastic gloves and then took my cane away, shoving an all-purpose lost-and-found wooden grandpa one into my naked hand instead, while I shivered out of my wheelchair to be scanned, randomly selected.

In the weeks that followed, our home school district struggled to find its sea legs. Online kindergarten was an exercise in cognitive dissonance, and then there was the matter of my child's voracious appetite for novelty. I thanked pre-hospital Santa for her foresight and redeemed the caterpillar coupon as quickly as I could.

Who doesn't love butterflies? Even my entomophobic

teenager found he could tolerate their fuzzy black larvae, so long as they would at no point be crawling on him personally.

It must be those wings, or at least the promise of them, that make the butterfly a "good bug." Butterfly wings are there to enchant us from the time we are babies on picnic blankets right on through our adult lives. I hung fabric birds and butterflies from my daughter's nursery ceiling. We sport wings on hand-bags, logos, sneakers, greeting cards. My aunt's risqué butterfly inner-thigh tattoo.

But it's not just about wings, is it? We love the story of the butterfly, one of the first science lessons we learn. In week one of Zoom school, they studied the life cycle, clicking through *Scholastic Magazine* articles and books read aloud by self-isolated celebrities. These are the first mysteries the elders let us in on: tadpole to frog; seed to tree; chrysalis, metamorphosis.

And she gobbles it up. To my daughter—still half-fey herself, still with fuzzy edges between real life and fantasy— the natural world is full of wonder, and life is beautiful.

IN MY DEFENSE, I did my due diligence, that first long week after they arrived. I read the brochure carefully—days to mature, minimum temperatures. I did the seasonal math. But I was also, at that point, a week into non-recovery. I forget words for things, and it's harder to type now; maybe my math skills suffered, too.

Also, Coronavirus Spring turned out to be much colder than expected.

Our Painted Ladies, on the other hand, did just what the tri-fold said they would. Over a span of days, we watched umpteen crawling commas balloon into long, ugly-cute grubs, like time-lapse in fast-forward, right before our eyes. We gawked at their first silk, their black underbellies. The silent, still cocoons.

Then suddenly, one morning . . . magic. But, not really.

Butterflies are a great metaphor for people who survive trauma. The symbolism soothes us. Butterflies represent hope, or at least a blueprint for how to move on. Trauma changes you, sometimes so much you don't recognize yourself. The butterfly says, *That's okay. Don't dwell. You have wings now.*

We had weeks of cold nights in quarantine, March to May. The instructions and the internet all said that butterflies don't survive below a certain temperature. Now I was a nursemaid to a moral dilemma. We named them, for god's sake. We paid to be part of the mystery of life, the chance to touch a metaphor, to launch a butterfly into blue skies and orgiastic blooms under a benevolent sun.

Where was the sun?

For every day that spring refused to come, we (and by "we" I mean "I") faced a new kind of math problem: how to balance the unfairness of weather against the tick-tock of little lives?

By week six they had long overstayed their welcome, but I took the obligation to heart. I gave them banana slices and juice-soaked cotton balls. I brought cuttings from the butterfly bush out back, to give their world texture and depth. I felt like Demeter, nurturing their instincts and appeasing my maternal guilt.

MOST PEOPLE DON'T KNOW that butterflies are actually noisy little fuckers. We assume they flit through the ether like angel's breath, but that, too, is delusion and hubris. By week seven of quarantine, I hated the sound of butterfly wings— that spasm of miniature panic against plastic.

The thud of a soft body falling.

What kills a butterfly, other than time, or teeth? The glossy pamphlet didn't have as much to say on this subject. Can a butterfly have cancer? Stroke? Can a butterfly know heartbreak?

I began to wonder if it's really fair to compare people to butterflies, all things considered.

The caterpillar's change is intragenic. It comes from within her; it's part of her narrative. Her life's urgent code.

In some people, too, trauma starts on the inside—a congenital weakness, in my case; an unfortunate stressor causing microscopic tears in my spinal dura, undetected and damaging as a gas leak for years and years, until a "Hail Mary" round of MRIs finally revealed that my cerebral tank is too low.

More often, human trauma comes from external forces, like —oh, pick one. The brutality of man on his own kind. The jaws of nature. Ill luck and happenstance. A day at the airport.

Either way, the key to being made better by trauma-as-chrysalis is to accept the story we were first given: that nature is as beautiful as it is awful. That there's balance, or better yet, purpose. That the caterpillar is not gone but different. That energy changes but is never lost.

I can accept that sometimes trauma changes us for the better. What doesn't kill us and all of that. For me the sticking point, though—the thing that keeps me up at night—is that the caterpillar *knows* how to become a butterfly, but can we say the same?

Does a person inherently know how to change? Even if she doesn't know she knows? Even if she never asked for it?

And if we do know, fundamentally, like the caterpillar, how to survive, adapt, evolve, does that mean people are designed to fall apart just to re-stitch themselves? Is the inevitability of trauma written in our genetic code?

I know plenty of people who took blows in life and never recovered. People who lived their "after" lives like liquid caterpillars in a person-husk. Where was their instruction manual? Are they the exception, or the rule?

Is evolution just something that happens, or doesn't, for no better reason than entropy?

———

DID you know that butterflies bleed when they emerge? Actually, it's "metabolic waste material," but a blood-red drip stain on snow-white habitat mesh is a quick way to disabuse a five-year-old that nature is anything like Disney. You can't even clean it, not without disturbing the wildlife. You may learn to look past it, but you'll never unsee it.

This was not in the booklet.

I was also told there would be no eggs, because butterflies only mate on specific plants, and only if they're in love and ask for consent. They lay their eggs on the plant and the babies eat the leaves and then come back as butterflies to pollinate it because there is balance.

But really nature is like *Jurassic Park*, in that life, uh, finds a way. With my backyard aptly named "butterfly" shrubs, I gave nature the car keys—but if I'm being perfectly honest, those hatchlings were going at it from the get-go, anyway. It's just that *the weather* kept them cooped up longer than the kit is meant for.

We ended up with a habitat full of wilting leaves and murky cotton balls and every other surface bejeweled with turquoise eggs as tiny as the knobby end of a butterfly's antenna. A speck in my daughter's palm.

And nature takes its course.

Butterfly corpses are weightless. Delicate. Their wings dissolve on your thumb.

But butterfly eggs are sturdy, all things considered. I spooned some into a jar as a countdown.

Maybe trauma, for humans, is more like a forest fire. Yes, fire clears a path for new life. Something good grows out of the wreckage. There is a cycle. But to those in its path, fire is just destruction.

Tell the blistered koala its sacrifice has meaning to the saplings.

Maybe the "survivor as butterfly" story is just religion. Maybe human trauma is just trauma: random, and devastating, to make of as you will. Even if we find a way to rebuild ourselves afterward, the loss of who we were is still a loss, and for every person who manages to recover, there's one who might never.

WHEN THE EGGS finally burst late in week eight, the jar became a riot, seething with minuscule lives.

It was time to let go.

We brought the habitat to the old raised garden bed where, before I got sick, I once grew herbs and marigolds and tomatoes for canning. Now it's overgrown with native shrubs, a butterfly's heaven. One by one, I gently caught the remaining Ladies, our true survivors (less than half) to be last-released into a pleasant, if breezy, May afternoon.

They were slow to rouse to their freedom. Sluggish in the fresh air, they hardly made a flutter in my palm. Most begrudgingly hopped to the nearest leaf, or the ground, just to sit there.

The sky was overcast. They called for rain all night, and then one last nice day before another freak snow front moved in.

At the end of our journey, all my daughter wanted was to hold a butterfly in that breathless moment, feel the long-anticipated tickle in her hand. All she really saw was the goodbye, and she got it. All the butterflies will now live forever in that moment in her memory. It's not for her to think about the quick vanishing into the robin's mouth her dad witnessed right after. She lost no sleep over the slow cold deaths that were coming.

Out of the half dozen butterflies we released that day, I only saw one actually fly away. It'd been the hardest to catch, too. Maybe it was the same one that had been fluttering like mad against the invisible cage, disturbing my thoughts for weeks. *That one* launched into the air as soon as the cave of my fingers opened—up over the neighbor's fence, it went, gone.

Maybe that anxious, damaged little bastard got to live out its remaining days doing what butterflies are supposed to do.

———

NOT LONG AFTER, Delaware announced the schools would remain closed for the rest of the school year. No news about summer camp. No word for my son, supposed to start high school in September. No way to know how long we'll be living our lives indoors. The pain in my head gets worse every day, while my daughter dances on the knife's edge of six, always wanting more.

But it's fine. We're . . . coping.

I don't feel like throwing myself up against the windows, beating my breast against what instinct tells me is a barrier, is wrong—yet. As if I could break through this virus spring just by force of will.

I believe there's a chance we can pull through this. The kids can't sleep at night while I dream of wings and wake up gasping. Is that a good omen, I wonder, or something else?

Are we butterflies?

LIFE SUPPORT

SUZANNE WEERTS

I am walking down the frozen food aisle in the grocery store. My glasses are fogged and I feel like I might hyperventilate into my mask. My cart is overflowing with food meant to last my family at least two weeks.

It is April 2020 and tensions are high. A figure is stopped in front of the ice cream freezer, maybe 50 feet ahead of me. The case closes, and I make out the shape of a woman heading in my direction, wearing purple gloves with angry eyes above her medical-grade mask, and she points at me. *"You're going the wrong way!"* she screams, and I search for how it is she knows this to be true and sure enough, there are arrows that I missed through my steam-filled glasses. We are the only people in the aisle. No one else witnesses her belligerence or my breakdown that follows. I lean against my surely COVID-covered cart and sob.

My life has become an endless cycle of cleaning and cooking and falling down the rabbit hole of news and numbers, statistics, and fear. The angry ice cream lady was right—I am going the wrong way. I was already questioning what I'd done with my one wonderful life when all of the things that I was doing came to a halt. A pandemic is not a good time for a midlife crisis. Or menopause. Hot flashes and masks don't mix. I've been known to tear off my sweater in the middle of a meeting, but you can't just rip off a face mask in the middle of Target.

Before the pandemic, I'd been plagued for several years with this nagging feeling that I wasted my life. That there was so much more I could have done with my potential and, well, I botched it.

For two decades, I've only worked part time. In essence, I've been on a 20-year maternity leave. It was a gift to be at home with my children and they turned out to be wonderful humans. But who knows, had I shared a medium-to-large part of that responsibility with a nanny or childcare center, perhaps I might have been a "contender" in some version of career success that eludes me now.

I'd planned to go back to work when the kids got into elementary school. We considered private schools, but after crunching the numbers, we figured that if I got involved at the local public school, maybe I could spend more time with my kids and use my event planning experience to make a difference. I figured I'd get a job when they moved on to middle school, but who wants to hire a woman in her 40s who's been out of the workforce for over a decade? I balked. I didn't even try. As the high school years stacked up, I let fear of failure get in the way. My nest had been empty for all of six months and I was plotting my next steps when COVID-19 closed the colleges and sent my birds back home for laptop learning.

That's when a bigger fear took hold. Bigger than the reality that I potentially wasted my life, my new fear is that I might also botch my death. I could die of COVID-19 and essentially disappear without saying goodbye. The poet Mark Nepo wrote, "At the bottom of every fear, when I could reach it, was my want not to die." The paralysis of my own fear keeps me mostly in my house, tense under the weight of all the recommended precautions. I'm not going the wrong way. I am going nowhere.

When my mother lost her battle with breast cancer over two decades ago, we were all by her bedside: her best friend, my siblings and my father. The white lights from the Christmas tree in her bedroom twinkled on the window panes while Irish music played and we held her hands as she gently faded away. It was serene, beautiful even, and I haven't feared death since my mother's conceivably choreographed departure.

But I unequivocally fear dying alone, and I fear that fate for my husband and other people dear to me, having their hands held by the latex-covered hands of a person they don't know. I fear that a goodbye to a ventilated parent on an iPad would haunt my children. And, should I be that person in that distant hospital bed, I fear leaving my husband to carry the emotional burden when emotion isn't something he is apt to indulge.

Many years ago, shortly after the birth of our first child, my husband and I wrote our wills. We planned for what would happen to our daughter should we die young. I told him that I'd like my ashes sprinkled half in the Atlantic Ocean, near where I was born, and the other half in the Pacific, where I spent so many of my best years. He joked that he could save a lot of money by simply flushing them down the toilet—after all, they'll end up in the same place.

When we got to the Do-Not-Resuscitate discussion, he immediately said, "No life support. Period." That concerned me. What if something happened to me and I was "in there" and could hear him talking but couldn't call out to let him know I am alert beyond the body on the bed, that there is still a chance I could make it? I added a clause to my portion of the will stating that my husband needed to get a second opinion from my friend Melanie. She is deeply religious and ever hopeful.

While I don't believe I'm necessarily going anywhere after I die, Melanie is certain that I am.

But I'm not ready now. I'm in the middle of a midlife crisis, which means I should have a few decades left. I may have written my will, but I haven't written my novel. I haven't seen my children discover their lives' paths nor have I figured out my own.

It is April 2021 and I am in the grocery store. The wire over my nose is expertly bent so that my mask doesn't cause my glasses to fog. Arrows no longer dictate my direction. A petite lady is standing in front of the peanut butter trying to reach a jar of jam on the top shelf. I ask if I can help. We are less than a foot apart, and she smiles in gratitude as I hand her the raspberry preserves. At least her eyes are smiling. It is these little things that tell me we're getting closer to normal. I no longer recoil if someone accidentally brushes against me as they pass in the aisle. I am craving hugs like I crave the oxygen seeping through the tight weave of my floral print mask.

Friends share photos of needles going into their arms and relieved smiles as they hold up CDC cards in social media posts. I want the peace of mind that seems to come with that. I want not to panic when my throat has a tickle or my chest feels tight. I want to put an end to my ventilator nightmares, and I want to get on with the next chapter of my one wonderful life.

People are creeping out of their cocoons and tentatively expanding their pods. I tell my husband maybe we should get the Johnson and Johnson vaccine. "The 'one-and-done' shot would mean we could see friends sooner," I say. The vaccinated are now the "cool kids" planning dinner parties and vacations. I'm an extrovert and a scheduler. My calendar has been empty for far too long. I want to be invited.

But my husband is an introvert. He hasn't minded the social ramifications of the pandemic. He suggests we get Moderna. It is a full six-week process from the first shot until full immunity. My husband has enjoyed that I no longer leave the house for evening meetings and all the charity events I used to RSVP for have gone virtual. He hasn't worn a suit in well over a year.

Of course, he is also one of those people who appreciated that the aftermath of 9/11 took away the option of showing up at the gate with a bouquet of flowers or hovering outside the gangway for tearful goodbyes. Curbside pick-up was always his preference, and for the last two decades he's been happy with his Uber-style grab-and-go version of "Have a safe trip" and "Welcome home." If social events could stay virtual post-pandemic, he'd be fine with logging on and then playing a video game in the other room. But that is not the direction I'm going.

For the first time in months, I am populating my calendar with plans. I have booked a few summer flights and we have hotel reservations. The kids' colleges are planning for in-person classes. There is a concert we may go to in the fall. And I have a job interview lined up. It's only part time, but it's a start.

DOING EVERYTHING RIGHT DURING THE PANDEMIC WAS WRONG FOR ME

ELIZABETH SUAREZ AGUERRE

We were well into the lockdown when we decided to make a run for it. After spending too many days watching news stories that looked more like the hazmat scene in *E.T.* than reality, my husband miraculously snagged a reservation at a campground that was still open, had private beach access, and promised plenty of space between sites.

I sat in the passenger seat of our motorhome, not in my usual relaxed, cross-legged, vacation-mode sort of way, but rigidly, with my back pressed straight up against the slightly worn cream leather and my feet firmly planted on the floor. I maintained a clichéd, but literal, white-knuckle death grip on my *Outlander, Book Six* novel. The familiar storylines within its million pages gave me a false sense of security; the characters were a connection to the normalcy we were living just weeks before, which now felt foreign and long ago.

I think I sat there, staring silently out the windshield at absolutely nothing, holding that book, heavy and grounding in my lap, for almost the entire six-hour drive. I don't think I even opened it. I just knew that I needed it, like an anchor. Its weight was the only thing keeping me from floating away into the apocalyptic feeling of panic I had been trying to subdue for two weeks. Little did I know that over the course of the next several months, I'd be replacing the weighty book with many other distractions in an attempt to maintain the suppression.

During those early pandemic days, people were either panic-buying toilet paper and paper towels, or they were scoffing and booking low fares to Europe. I remained somewhere in the middle. Although I was a little fearful of what I was seeing on the news, I thought: "Something like that is never going to happen *here*. It *can't* happen. They won't let it." Who, exactly, was I referring to? Who were these unseen forces that I thought, in my incredibly ignorant bliss, would control and take care of things the way they were "supposed" to?

I paid a little more attention to the news and washed my hands a bit more often, but I went on with my life and my plans without a particularly high level of concern. In fact, mere days before the lockdown, my friend and I were comparing our packing lists for the cruise our two families were going on the following week. We were at a local school gymnasium watching our sons compete in an engineering robotics tournament. It would turn out to be their last school event.

The gym was filled with the whirring and buzzing of student-made robots, mixed with the occasional cheers and chants of dozens of preteens. Noisy adult chatter that usually consisted of small talk about the kids and the weather was replaced with virus gossip. When my friend and I learned at team check-in that two of our sons' classmates did not attend due to "safety concerns," we rolled our eyes. We were sitting on the bleachers, discussing how many bathing suit cover-ups we needed, when one of the moms leaned in over our shoulders and asked if we were *really* still planning on going and *weren't we scared?* We dismissed her and returned to our debate on the best ways to smuggle booze onto the ship in our suitcases.

The very next week, we watched and listened as the world slowly began to shut down, phase by phase, and I slowly started to fall apart, piece by piece.

AT EACH STAGE of the lockdown, I felt a new surge of panic. First, it was the schools—just an extra week off before Spring Break. Then it was the bars, the restaurants, and non-essential businesses—just until this sinister curve was magically flattened. The day I found out that our neighborhood beach and boardwalk were closed (as in, actually closed with police cars blocking the roads, lights whirling), I felt like I was trapped in some sort of bizarre sci-fi movie.

The feelings of panic, fear, and anxiety were so intense in that moment that I could physically feel them consuming me, bubbling up from my toes, my legs, and into my lungs. I truly believed that if I allowed myself to process this, to think about it, to accept it as reality, I would have a complete and total breakdown. So, instead, I poured myself another cocktail, refused to acknowledge it, and metaphorically covered my ears: "La, la, la, la! I'm not *listening!*"

During the last year, I did everything the articles, therapists, and well-meaning friends recommended. I diligently recited at least three things I was grateful for each day. I self-assigned three DIY home projects per week. I Googled "no-gym-required fitness routines" and power walked in my neighborhood more in a few months than I had in five years. I created a list of "fun" and "engaging" activities and called it "Quarantine Whimsy."

Perhaps if I titled it something light and fluffy, it really would be. It's still there in my Notes app—31 items ranging from "Drink wine" to "Sand and stain wood counters." (The wine item was checked off repeatedly. The counters are still scratched and dull.) I don't know if I am saving my list so I can remember the things we did to get through that time period, or if I'm keeping it "just in case" we need it again. I'm not sure if I trust the world anymore.

Each time the panic threatened to creep in, I refused to allow it entrance. I would turn to my list, go outside, open a beer, or shop online for essential items, such as, "Quarantine Hair Don't Care" ball caps. I recently found a page in one of my journals with the sentence "The world is coming undone and I don't want to talk about it." It was written in a messy, rushed script diagonally across the entire page. I suspect I thought if I wrote it down, I could force-eject that cassette tape out of my head, violently yanking out the ribbon so it could not play over and over again. I thought that would help. It didn't.

Somewhere around December, I started to break down slowly and subtly. I was moody (okay, even moodier than my non-pandemic normal self). I became ridiculously impatient and developed an obnoxious habit of interrupting every sentence my husband started. I got sick. I yelled at my kids (more). I ended my birthday, which had been a perfectly lovely family camping trip, by crying hysterically.

My kids had woken me with presents and singing. We went out for brunch at a cute, little local spot. We mountain-biked for miles along the swooping, wooded trails in the national forest near our campground. Even my 15-year-old son had worn the pink and purple birthday hat on top of his helmet, the elastic string stretched taut, digging in under his chin. After dinner, I made a wish as I blew out the candle in my gooey s'more.

A sparkly birthday banner was taped to the outside of our motorhome and my husband had strung up twinkling Christmas lights along the RV's awning and over the hood. When the boys had showered and gone in to watch movies for the night, I turned to kiss my husband and the sentence "Worst birthday ever!" fell out of my mouth.

Even I was surprised by the words. Where had they come from? Why would I say that? In actuality, it had been a really good birthday: fun, simple, sweet, and filled with my three favorite people. But it ended with me sitting in my foldable camping chair—staring at the crackling fire, whiskey glass in hand, hot tears pouring down my cheeks—feeling remorseful, ungrateful, and sad.

Several weeks later, as New Year's Eve approached, it seemed as if the world was holding its breath, hoping, against logic, that by putting 2020 away, relief would finally arrive. I didn't think anything would change on January 1st, so I was surprised when I woke up that first morning of the new year with an even stronger sense of despair and disappointment.

I was so damned tired of "making the best of" every cancelled event and situation that I damaged myself somewhere along the way. I spent all those months trying to go against my nature to cry and scream and whine and roll my anxieties into a giant snowball of irrational "what-ifs." But I realized that it wasn't just because I thought if I allowed myself to cry, I wouldn't be able to stop. It was my deep, subconscious fear that if I did not constantly and actively acknowledge that *Everything is fine! We are so lucky! We are so grateful!*, then maybe The Universe would put me in my place: "What's that you say? You're miserable? Depressed? Frustrated? Hold my beer." We knew that we were the lucky ones. I might have lost my sanity, but we had not lost our jobs or our loved ones. I felt like I had no right to complain.

Instead, I focused on what I could do to make the best of everything and stay positive. Ironically, by trying to do everything that the mental health experts advised, I ended up feeling more trapped, frustrated, and panicked, and less in control. I did everything right. I did okay. I survived. But I still fell apart. I realize now it would have been healthier to have allowed myself to admit how scared and frustrated I was, instead of thinking that giving in to my emotions was going to make me give up. There was no book heavy enough to suppress the feelings I needed to acknowledge.

My heart is kind of like those kitchen counters I never got to: a little scratched and a little dull. I worry that this necessary, temporary, social distancing is making us all permanently emotionally disconnected. I am starting to see and feel some hope, but I'm going to keep that list of whimsy on my phone. I'm not sure if it is a souvenir or insurance, but either way, I'll keep making the best of things . . . *and* allow myself some tears and crazy along the way.

WHALE SONG

REBECCA ATKINSON

The baby wakes in the night and I go to him. He is in his own room, a toddler bed lined up next to his sister's single, because he's not really a baby anymore. But still, he wakes every few hours and cries out for me.

Tonight his chest heaves with sobs. "I want my whale! Where my whale?"

I look around the dark room, at the soft shapes of discarded cuddly toys, splayed picture books, and tiny heaps of dirty clothes. "What whale?" I ask him, even though he's barely awake. "Sshhh, you'll wake your sister. What whale?"

"Big whale," he screams in my face.

Then I remember the postcard that arrived that morning from my mother—a shiny black and white killer whale leaps out of the sea towards the camera. It came with her *National Geographic* magazine, and she sent it on to us, along with some radish seeds and new coloring pens.

I race downstairs and rip the postcard off the fridge, and bring it to him, my baby. He clutches it to his chest and falls back asleep until morning.

This is just the beginning. We scroll through *Paw Patrol* and

Octonauts on the Amazon box, searching for episodes that have whales in them. We watch videos on YouTube of orcas swimming, hunting, breaching choppy waters.

The shops are closed, the libraries too, so I buy books online. My best friend in Florida sends us a whale key ring, which we quarantine for 72 hours, then another 12, just to be sure. Once opened, I clip it to the buggy for him to admire during our daily walk around the block. We celebrate his second birthday at home, just the four of us, and the night before, I wrap overpriced wooden toys and a beluga-shaped cushion that he can take to bed with him at night.

We learn their names. Orcas, blue whales, and humpbacks are his favourites. But there are also sperm whales, minke whales, fin whales. The Southern right whale, very endangered. The mysterious Omura's whale. Beluga, Bryde's, and bowhead whales—the names roll off your tongue like salt water.

We discover that whale sharks are fish, not whales, but we love them anyhow because they are peaceful and calm, and the females give birth to up to 300 babies at a time.

Narwhals are a strange one. "They are whales," I tell him, but he laughs and shakes his head.

"That not a whale mummy, that a narwhal."

And how do you argue with such logic?

His sister is put out. She wants a favorite animal to obsess over. She decides maybe lions are her thing, but after some brief research she moves on to seals. We Google different types. There are a lot. She asks for a cuddly seal toy, and I tell her to put it on her Christmas list. It is still spring, and already we know that it's going to be a long year.

After the kids go to bed, I prep for the next day. Print off coloring sheets and writing exercises. I cry on the sofa while I watch the news, and pour another glass of wine.

My husband sets up an office in our bedroom and closes the

door. I audit the fridge and sit in online waiting rooms, trying to book food deliveries. I get out tubs of play dough, jigsaw puzzles, Legos, building blocks. I tidy them away again.

We make banana bread and then eat it in the warmth of our tiny yard. It's 11 a.m. and I am exhausted. We watch Disney films, and make obstacle courses out of sofa cushions, and wish away the time.

My mother video calls us. The kids pretend to be ninjas in the background, and I can barely make out what she is saying.

"I think it's a boy thing," I hear between shrieks. "When I was teaching, all the boys used to obsess over things. Normally trains or buses. I don't expect he's seen many of those."

"He's seen buses, Mum," I say, loudly. "And I don't think boys have a monopoly on being into stuff. I'm worried he might be autistic?"

"Don't be silly, he's just two."

We lose connection, so I call her back on the landline.

"Isn't it funny that he should be so into whales when you live so far from the sea," she says.

I imagine home—her home I mean, but it was mine too once upon a time—where, if you open the top bedroom window and stick your head right out, you can catch the sparkle of the English Channel.

The sea is too far away for us to visit, it's not allowed anymore. I think maybe we will take a day trip when restrictions are lifted—paddling, ice cream, collecting sea glass. My son will watch the waves and spot something in-between crests.

"A whale, it a whale," he will shout, and we will pretend to see it too and take a photo.

What is it about them that attracts him so much? At first, all I see are their sausage-rolled bodies, squashed together then stretched from head to tail. Though they breathe the same air as us, they are too big to survive on land—it is only the buoyancy of the sea that prevents a whale's organs from being crushed by its own body weight.

I find it hard to believe they are mammals at all, and I buy myself a book about the evolution of animals. I plan to read it, maybe when schools reopen.

But secretly, I am proud that he loves whales and not buses or trains. What's so interesting about a bus? He must have something of the sea in him—born in the caul on a hospital corridor floor, the midwife later told me it meant he would be protected from drowning.

Precious and feared. Deadly and vulnerable. I read how whales learned to fight back against the ships of men sent to kill them. How they are known to play and to grieve. They birth and nurse and raise their young at sea. I start to feel an affinity too.

AT NIGHT, I lie in bed and imagine I am deep in the ocean. Weightless in the dark, I glide slowly through blue peace. Just the rustle of sand and clicking of giant sea creatures. I sink into coldness then rise for air, sink and rise.

My son cries out for me, but it's morning, and he's slept through the night. I hear his sister wake and comfort him, picking his special cushion off the floor and turning the light on.

"I'll get up with them this morning," my husband says, rolling out of bed.

I have no idea what day it is, but it hardly matters anyhow. I close my eyes and go back to sleep to the sound of whales singing.

IT TOOK A PANDEMIC TO CONVINCE MY MOTHER I'M ENOUGH

JOAN DELCOCO

When Caller ID announces my mother is on the line, I brace for the headache I know will come. She shout-talks into her speakerphone and doesn't hear me unless I shout-talk back, so our conversations sound and feel like altercations.

"What are you doing?"

"We're eating."

"Why are you eating so late?"

"It's seven, Ma. We always eat at seven."

"Do you know I'm 93? You expect me to remember what time you eat?"

My hackles rise, but I know it's foolish to take the bait. I say, evenly, "No one expects you to remember, Ma. You asked what we were doing, so I told you."

"You always have to have the last word, don't you?"

Damn, she's good. Ninety-three, and she can still blindside me. She manufactures disagreements and won't back down until she gets me to say, "I'm sorry, you're right."

But I won't indulge her tonight. I don't have the cognitive or emotional bandwidth to engage with her on the small stuff. This relentless daily striving of keeping us all safe is draining, and I operate on a deficit to begin with because I have a traumatic brain injury.

And, though I'm embarrassed to admit it, the petty skirmishes my mother so relishes can trigger decades-old vulnerabilities. She is right and I am wrong: that was always the price for her love and approval.

Assuaging her need for affirmation costs me little now, but I paid dearly trying to appease her in my younger years. Endlessly begging her forgiveness for sins unnamed or imagined, making myself quiet and small to escape her critical eye and excoriating tongue.

Or, even worse, the dreaded silent treatment. If I dared to speak my mind or show my unworthiness by acting out of turn, she'd ignore me out of existence.

It took me decades to construct an autonomous self, gain confidence, learn to assert my needs in the wider world. Yet even now, when she is upset for reasons I cannot change, the pull of her need can knock me off kilter and send me into a tailspin, trying to make things right for her.

Because I am not okay if she's not.

I do everything she asks and more; I anticipate and accommodate my parents' every need—for groceries, medical attention, entertainment, affection. I remind my grown kids to call them regularly. She'll just have to live with that.

In the seconds I don't reply now, I hear the grumble of her frustration from deep in her gullet, like a cat trying to clear a fur ball. Before, this would've quickly escalated to full-throated invective, but age and infirmity and a global pandemic have altered that.

She's got far more pressing concerns. Like keeping my 94-year-old father with dementia safe and tethered to his identity while they're imprisoned in a one-bedroom apartment.

My mother counts on me to acknowledge her frustrations

and devotion, to admire her ingenuity at outsmarting the wily combatant that would've stolen more of my father away if not for her vigilance.

I talk her back from the edge when her threadbare patience is about to snap. Which is often. She's a native New Yorker; patience is *not* in her DNA.

I take a deep breath, pop a Tylenol, call on my better angels, and summon the right degree of brightness as I listen to her running commentary: "He's sleeping too much . . . he didn't offer to help with the dishes . . . he started that new jigsaw puzzle!"

Then follow exhaustive descriptions of his intakes of the meals she's diligently served, and, God help me, of his outputs . . .

I supply "uh-huhs" and "yeahs" as needed, suppressing responses she won't hear: it's okay for him to sleep till 11; it's unrealistic to expect his help with chores; he's not doing any of this deliberately.

I relax some as I sense her cheering up. At least he's eating— at least they both are. A couple of times when her exhaustion and helplessness at what my father won't or can't do have exceeded her depleted coping skills, my mother's gone "on strike."

I was horrified when I realized this meant they were subsisting on cold cereal; I cooked up a storm and rushed over there toting bags of nutritious meals. Only to be met with scolding that I shouldn't "fuss."

A day or two later, she'd reported he was "better." He'd poured his own orange juice. Yelled back when she nagged him to talk more, even threatening to leave and inching his walker towards the door.

"You see?" she exclaimed. "He can still do things if he wants. I just have to motivate him."

That time, I was silent for his sake. I understood her frustration; my body vibrated with her pain. But I couldn't encourage her perverse thinking, that if she did less, he'd magically understand that he needed to do more, the way it worked between them for 70-plus years.

My mother's resilience is magnificent but grievously flawed: she makes the best of her reality, and when reality bests her, she invents a parallel universe in which she holds sway. A narrative in which she can "motivate" my fading father out of his "bad moods." She resists hearing that some days he can do more than others, and refuses to concede his cognitive decline isn't linear. Because she won't fully accept the truth of his impairment.

But even her most deft maneuvers can't jolt him back to being the man who took care of her. And though she yells at her television, she can't persuade those who ignore or willfully spread the virus that their actions extend her time in hell.

Tonight she bears her troubles more lightly, though, and says, "He's a pain in the neck. He's sitting right here—I'm just saying that to get a rise out of him."

And he fires back a rare retort that reminds us he's still himself. "Oh yeah? Show me which side the pain is on."

And they laugh, because there is comfort in this familiar back-and-forth, exchanges of kindnesses and acts of service, wrapped up tight in harsh words and raised voices: their love language for almost three-quarters of a century.

My daughter, who overhears every shouted word, sees my moist eyes and brushes her lips against my hair. She knows I'm thinking he was doing much better when we visited regularly; we should be doing more; Grandma needs help.

I voice these concerns, but my mother brushes them off. "No, I don't want the risk, I can still manage." But we both know this is barely true. Her sharp intake of breath tells me she's doing what I'm doing: uttering our daily silent prayer that they can outlast the danger.

Our conversation seems to be winding down when she remembers what she'd meant to share at the outset. "Guess who remembers how to sew?"

Soon my daughter is misty-eyed, too, as Grandma describes coaxing Grandpa to resuscitate their ancient factory-model Singer sewing machine. How muscle memory we thought long gone kicked in, and there he was, suddenly her valiant partner on the mission that's consumed her for months—making masks for our family. She has spent hours raging at and braving the mysteries of Google and YouTube, searching for the perfect pattern and instructions.

"He sews straighter than me," she crows. Over the years, they've sewn curtains, doll clothes and costumes for their grand-children, but he hasn't touched a machine since his stroke 15 years ago.

Now they're a team again, twisted hands and dimmed eyes cheating death with scissors, pins, floral wire, elastic, tightly-woven cotton, and the old Singer machine.

She's tired, but replenished. "I gotta go," she says, her customary sign-off, though now she goes nowhere, ever. And then, her newer closing: "I love you."

"I love you too," I say, still surprised each time I hear her say it. She has said these words loudly and often to her grandchil-dren for years, but less freely to me.

For after six decades of getting it wrong, it seems I have finally learned to be the daughter she always needed me to be. She pours into that one word, "love," everything she has long withheld, so that I feel her heart speaking to mine. Telling me she accepts me as an adult who offers her care and succor, and cherishes my devotion. I'm a good daughter. I am enough.

DURING THE PANDEMIC, I have been writing to make sense of the world, rewire my brain, reclaim my voice, and define my post-injury self. When I began writing about my relationship with my mother, I hoped to rescue the girl who was beaten down by her mother's words and silences but never felt entitled to express or own her anger. Adult, brain-injured me had anger enough for both of us, and I was ready to exact some retribution, if only on my computer screen.

But as I revisit our history in a present when every fiber strains for loving connection, past hurts have become irrelevant. The narrative arc of our mother-daughter story has pulled me away from anger, towards radical compassion for my mother. I understand that her harshness and withholding were toxic byproducts of her need to exercise some control in a life that offered painfully few choices.

And I cannot deny the haunting parallels between us. I, too, have been less than my children needed me to be, when the pain and limitations of my TBI were beyond what I could handle. I know we cannot nurture well when we are not whole.

I need to absolve my mother, not indict her, if it's healing and connection I am after.

Now when I write, I am burning to use my revived voice and shiny new words to bear witness to the pathos of my parents' daily struggles. To pay tribute to the poignant beauty of our familial bonds, however messy.

To celebrate that my mother and I have finally gotten the knack of loving each other.

I don't know what I will do when she is gone.

SLEEP LIKE A MIDLIFE WOMAN

JENNIFER LANG

Embark on a needless trip to the bathroom. After slipping back into bed, begin nightly mantra—*I will fall [back] to sleep, I will fall [back] to sleep, I will fucking fall [back] to sleep.*

Regret skipping YouTube yoga, a feeble attempt to lubricate your stiff spine and tire out your tight hips.

Wonder what time it is but do not check. Do *not* turn on the phone. Do *not*!

Wonder what day it is since they blur into one another, since lockdown number three started two weeks ago, since a global pandemic became your surreal new normal 324 days ago.

Pull up weighted blanket to neck and lie on your back in Savasana with legs splayed, feet pronated. Husband loves the ten-pound blanket—a belated birthday present from your three children—like a pet but you worry if ten pounds is too weighted on your petite frame. Think about what weighs you down: Ilan the acupuncturist's casual comment about weak kidney pulse, Dr. Yahini's nonchalant question about high cholesterol and heart disease, memories of Uncle Sid parading you around his eccentric neighborhood in Venice Beach and driving up north to visit, his banana-colored clunky diesel Mercedes announcing his arrival.

Listen to snoring spouse. A warbling canary? Spouting whale? Erupting volcano? Praise old college roommate who recommended the heavy-duty fluorescent yellow and fuchsia foam earplugs, specially designed for construction workers, as you squeeze, twist, insert, and feel foam expand like an eardrum orgasm.

Bring on yoga breath. Inhale 1, 2, 3, 4, 5. Exhale 10, 9, 8, 7, 6, 5, 4, 3, 2, 1.

Question if sudden temperature changes are par for the course at 55 or if kidneys really are not functioning right. Shove aside blanket to avoid menopausal asphyxiation.

Conclude it's a whale. Nudge husband with more force than necessary.

Think about Netflix, nightly savior for the past 11 months. Think about *The Crown*. Think about the Queen. Remember scenes where Elizabeth and Philip bid one another goodnight before heading to separate bedrooms and feel something akin to jealousy as your spouse spurts.

Curse yourself for missing the yogic antidote for insomnia: lying on your back, outstretched arms, bolster under butt, and legs up the living room wall.

Ponder your to-do list: read stories for literary magazine, plan writing workshop, query memoir, research new Netflix series since you've finished *Lupin*, *Firefly Lane*, and *Monarca*, calculate best time to call mother ten hours behind in California, invent non-essential ingredients for lentil soup to ensure a big outing, two blocks east, to Victory.

Picture your mother's big brother and only sibling, Uncle Sid, at your wedding 30 years earlier in Israel, dead of a massive heart attack three months later in Los Angeles and stuck in time at age 59. Fret if occasional achy legs and full-body fatigue are heart-related. Brood about big yellow bruise on shin and possible leukemia onset. Is coronavirus making you crazy or have you always been like this? By day, spouting husband says the latter.

Weigh pros and cons of packing up pillow and sleeping in guest room: not your bed, but dark and quiet.

To tiptoe back to the bathroom to pop an Ambien or Calms Forté, Benadryl or BHI Calming Tablet, or not to tiptoe, that is one of so many questions?

Recite friend-recommended yogic ABC: A is for Astavakrasana, B for Baddha Konasana, C for Chaturanga Dandasana, D for Dhanurasana. Keep going. Focus. Strive to think of a pose for every letter of the alphabet, your own anti-Alzheimer's exercise to escape your father's fate.

Realize that if you escape your father's fate, surely you will face a different one like kidney failure, leukemia, heart attack, or some other ghastly end.

Chastise yourself: Is it normal to obsess over your mortality in the middle of the night? In the middle of your life?

Remember your mother telling you long ago, perhaps high school, maybe college, that there's no such thing as normal, especially now as the world careens and caroms out of control.

Spread-eagle yourself on the crisp, clean sheets. Pretend you're flying in clouds or floating on water. Fall asleep without fully appreciating it.

LIFE AND DEATH OF AN ANGRY CHIHUAHUA

KIMI CERIDON

Typically, my husband and I walk a quarter of a mile to the vet's office for appointments, but today, my husband drives me over with Chili, a seven-pound Chihuahua, in my lap. Chili is not in pain, at least as far as I can tell—no wincing, no shaking, no whining. In fact, he seems content with me cradling him, stroking his back. That's how I know he's not feeling well.

Massachusetts instituted a mask mandate and restricted indoor activities in March, so visits to the vet require extra precautions. I had called the vet to ask how they administered euthanasia given the restrictions. The vet's COVID-safe procedure in April was for the owner to hand their pet to a technician on the office's front steps. The last time the owner would see their pet would be as the technician walked it through the front door.

At 21, Chili is old, even for a Chihuahua. He's never been one of those palm-size, bug-eyed, teacup Chihuahuas that starlets use as accessories. His little Russet potato-shaped body perches on four spindly stilts. I think he looks like those AT-AT walker robots from the Star Wars movies. Add a coat of blonde fur, a bat-like face, and sharp, pointed ears to make Chili's perfect doppelganger.

Chili was my mom's dog. She died in 2016 without leaving instructions for his care. Her last will and testament had few instructions about money or property, so it was no surprise Chili was not mentioned either. My older brother, younger sister, and I had many opportunities to talk about these things while we were together at her bedside during the last two weeks of her life. But my family is good at avoiding adult responsibility conversations, preferring to lean hard on the adage, "Things will work out for the best somehow."

During my mom's chemotherapy treatments, she lived with my sister. Chili was part of the move-in package. So, my brother and I shirked responsibility for Chili by flying away after my mom passed. We just assumed my sister would keep him. I'd like to blame grief for my ambivalence, but honestly, I never liked Chili. And the only person Chili liked was my mother.

When Mom adopted Chili, two families had already previously adopted him. They returned him after he had snapped at their kids. Even though he was deemed unadoptable, a family friend asked if my mom was interested in a Chihuahua with a bad attitude. "Ewww," my mom said. "Aren't Chihuahuas ugly little useless dogs that people carry around in purses?" Then she wrinkled her brow, rolled her eyes, and stuck out her tongue in disgust.

I'm not sure how she went from that reaction to Chili moving in; I think she couldn't bear letting the shelter put down even an ugly dog. Lousy attitude aside, as soon as Chili arrived, he adored my mom. He followed her around the house, inches off her heels. If she stood still, he'd tilt his head up and gaze at her in silent worship.

The first time I met Chili, I walked through my mom's front door, and before I crossed the threshold, he let loose on me. He barked with a high-pitched yap and darted in and out of my legs, snapping at my ankles. I giggled at his antics until he lifted his leg and peed on my shoe.

Chili refused to be reformed no matter how much my mom tried training him. He had no interest in befriending his human siblings—my brother, sister, or me. If anyone got near him, he'd fixate his beady, black eyes on them, snarl, and bare his teeth. He'd snap at anyone close enough. Chili once sunk one of his sharp, needle-like teeth into the tender skin between my husband's thumb and forefinger. As blood spurted from the wound, Chili wiggled out of my husband's grasp and hid behind my mom's legs.

Parked curbside, I call the vet. When they tell me I can come in, I lift Chili out of my lap. There are no snarls or snaps. He folds himself into my arms and buries his head in the crook of my elbow. It seems sweet, but I know his friendliness means he doesn't have any fight left in him.

My mom reciprocated Chili's adoration with long, one-sided conversations. He'd listen intently, tilting and cocking his head at the right moments. He hopped into her lap every time she sat down to watch television. She'd automatically start scratching his forehead, and he'd close his eyes and gurgle. On daily walks, Chili padded along beside my mom, and he rode shotgun everywhere she drove. He also flew all over the country tucked under an airplane seat. Somehow he knew better than to be nasty to TSA agents.

During the last two weeks of my mom's life, Chili never left the end of her bed. If anyone interrupted his vigil to take him out, he growled, then immediately returned to his spot. My siblings and I thought it was a sign of his old age. After all, he was already 17. Then, hours before my mom drew her last breath, Chili hopped off her bed, walked into the family room, and curled up in his dog bed by the television.

Chili moved in with my husband and me a year and a half ago. My sister asked me to take care of him because her oldest had health issues and Chili was too much work. When I thought, "Things will work out for the best somehow," I suppose I had expected Chili to die not long after my mom had. It never occurred to me that a bustling household with a newborn and a toddler probably wasn't the best home for an angry, geriatric dog.

Twenty-one years haven't tempered Chili's attitude, but they have slowed him down and dulled his teeth. His hind legs are stiff with arthritis. He is deaf, and cataracts have clouded what's left of his eyesight. When he's not curled up in his dog bed, he ambles around the first floor of my house, bumping into things or getting stuck in the legs of furniture. I started an Instagram account to post photos of his dilemmas—a silly tribute to my furry sibling. Oh yeah, Chili also can't retract his penis. I mention this tidbit because telling people that my husband lovingly lubricates his little pink appendage with Vaseline brings comedic relief to an otherwise sad situation.

My husband and I contemplated putting Chili down for months. We knew 21 in dog years was old. Despite his Instagrammable escapades, Chili was a champ at beating odds.

COVID arrived in March, but come April, Chili's once razor-like teeth were falling out, and his breath smelled of rot and death. He was too old for surgical extraction, but we thought antibiotics would help with the pain. We walked to the vet, handed Chili over to a technician at the front door, and waited for a vet to call. She scolded us about Chili's care before finally offering the prescription. The whole debacle left us uncomfortable with surrendering Chili curbside to be put to death, so we postponed any talk of euthanasia.

Just days after we finished the prescription, the rotting breath returned. I hoped Chili would pass in his sleep, and we could avoid COVID-style euthanasia. I also wanted Chili to be comfortable until the end. I guess his two decades had softened my sharp edges too. We had the prescription refilled three more times before I asked about putting him down again.

As of July, one person could be with Chili when he died. It wasn't ideal, but I made the appointment anyway.

The technician ushers me into the exam room directly across from the office's front door. The vet is already there. She reaches across the divide to hand me a laminated brochure. It's cremation information. The pictures of wooden boxes and urns suddenly remind me of a similar box that held my mom's remains. I remember how much my mom loved Chili and suddenly putting him down feels like losing her all over again. Fresh tears roll down my cheeks and soak the top of my cotton mask.

A technician muzzles Chili's tiny snout to administer the first sedative. Chili lies down, and they remove the muzzle. The vet administers a fatal dose of phenobarbital, then she and the technician retreat into the office, leaving me with Chili. I blink back tears, longing for my husband to be next to me. I would squeeze his hand, hoping his touch would stop my brain from flooding with memories of my mother on her deathbed. Instead, I reach down and stroke Chili's head as he takes his last breath. Then, I am alone.

A GARDEN OF GRATITUDE LILIES

ANDRA WATKINS

For the first two months of the pandemic, I was like most people. I washed my anxious hands incessantly. Stockpiled toilet paper. Bought all the yeast. Baked all the bread. Ate all the bread. I went from traveling the country two weeks a month and meeting thousands of people to self-isolation, gaining ten carb-fueled pounds, and sleeping until noon.

At 51, I was effectively unemployed, a certified failure.

A steady source of income vanished with the onset of March 2020. My work relied on travel, planes, and speaking in person to strangers whose breath might now kill me. Instead of clamoring to meet new people, the pandemic forced me to view every human being as a potential Grim Reaper, a fear that grew stronger and deepened my isolation. As one of the millions of American women with compromised immunity, I didn't know what this vicious novel disease might do to me, and I was determined not to find out.

Because my chronic illness is invisible, I've learned not to talk about ailments others can't see. Our culture trains women to keep struggles to themselves, especially those of us above a certain age. We're exaggerating. Having a pity party. Going through menopause. We need to see another therapist or swallow another pill. Every cry for help is calling attention to our fading glory as it sparks out like a defective firework—a situation we are expected to endure with humbleness, submission, and most of all, silence. Defeated, cut off from my friends, and lonely during the pandemic, I hunkered down in my house, ate more bread, rationed more toilet paper, and slept myself into severe depression.

How could I expect anyone to care about my struggles? The entire world weathered the same losses: loss of freedom, loss of health, loss of income, loss of loved ones, loss of unscheduled time, loss of life. I couldn't share my negative energy with anyone, because everyone had ample burdens to bear.

Once I decided it wasn't healthy to sleep all day, I forced myself to face my altered reality. Nobody was going to rescue me. Only I could give myself what I needed. Little by little, I started to cope, but my hands continued to be a problem. I manifest nervous energy through my hands: the more agitated I am, the more frantic my hands become. Some days, I had to sit on my hands to keep them still for a few minutes. As soon as I released them, my hands motored into projects, like two overactive sets of helicopter blades thrashing through every room.

Desperate for a positive outlet for my hand movement, I found a dusty stack of origami paper and began folding sheets into lilies. A lily stands for peace, but I hadn't considered the flower's meaning. I liked to fold origami lilies because they are a complicated four-petaled flower that took skill, precision, and time. The impressive results felt like an accomplishment. On fraught days, I made dozens.

For a couple of months, careful creasing and movement lifted my spirits. I filled decorative bowls with my creations, wove them into tacky leis, and perched them in my ratty pandemic hair. I left them under my husband's pillow and stuffed them into random nooks and niches, hoping their discovery might make another struggling person's day.

My husband was happy to see me occupied with something positive, but he is a modernist minimalist architect. Translated, he is a man who dislikes clutter, especially floral clutter. My frilly handiwork marred the clean lines of our sofa and destroyed the mojo of our concrete walls and ceilings. Twitching from an overload of Eastern-themed Victoriana, he demanded to know my intentions for the riotous garden of paper flowers sprouting all over the house. When the pandemic was over, would rescue workers break down our door and find our dead bodies beneath ten feet of origami lilies?

Around the same time, John Oliver, host of HBO's *Last Week Tonight*, released a set of limited-edition postage stamps to raise money for the U.S. Post Office. At the urging of a friend, I bought four sheets. Eighty stamps. What on earth would I do with 80 stamps when I pay bills online and send an occasional card or thank-you note?

I considered letter-writing. I could use cool John Oliver stamps to pen old-fashioned letters to people in my life. Maybe one of my missives would find someone at her lowest, and it would fuel her through another interminable pandemic day. Or someone might open his mailbox and discover joy instead of bills and junk mail. But I didn't have acceptable stationery. For me, card and stationery shopping is a tactile experience. I want to touch and stroke and smell every option, a fix I don't get from browsing online. It wasn't safe to visit the local paper and card shop. I'm no designer. I couldn't style my own paper.

Or could I?

I eyed my pile of five-inch square origami sheets, their gold leaves, rich reds, vibrant blues. A pristine white side was meant to be folded inward. I selected the paper on top, found my best pen, and started writing. And thus blossomed my pandemic panacea—an outpouring of lilies of gratitude.

Daily from May to November 2020, every reason I had to be grateful for each recipient streamed onto pieces of origami paper. I folded these offerings into ornate lilies, letter-side in. Each lily I mailed included a card explaining the project because I wanted to be sure people would unfold the flower and read their letter. I left each flower flat, placed it in a small craft paper envelope with handwritten instructions, sealed the package into a white mailing envelope, and slapped a John Oliver stamp on the outside.

Running out of John Oliver stamps didn't stop the flow of gratitude lilies to friends, acquaintances, and inspirations. Below are extracts.

To John Oliver: *Thank you for teaching me things we desperately need to learn and for inspiring this project.*

To a former fellow art resident: *Because of you, I left Portugal with several new friends, but more crucially, you gave me a new way to see.*

To Barack Obama: *I'm sorry I never voted for you, but I'm on your side now. Even world leaders need pick-me-ups.*

To Jen Mann, a fellow author: *For someone who brands herself a raging, blunt (and hilarious) woman, you are one of the most generous souls I've met on this long road.*

To Jennifer Lawrence: *You are an inspiration to creators like me. Fearless. Uncompromising. You crack the creative universe open and help us glimpse the divine.*

To Dr. Fauci: *Leaders say the hard things nobody wants to hear. They tirelessly seek a way forward, even through the meanest adversity. Thank you for saving lives.*

I don't know whether most recipients read their lilies. A few people reached out to tell me what it meant to them, but knowing their impact wasn't the point. Telling people why I was thankful for them caused me to dwell on gratitude and reminded me I have hundreds of reasons to be grateful. Every day, as I penned another message, I considered what I had instead of everything I lost. Enough souls impacted my life to write daily for over six months. Sometimes, I wrote several lilies a day because thankfulness came easily. But when it didn't, I was always able to find a glimmer of gratitude, however tenuous at first. I started with a few stubborn words, and on my darkest days, words became sentences until they filled the page and lifted me.

Gratitude lilies also shifted my overall attitude: I looked for the positive in the worst news, focused on quiet moments without the blare of outrage and death, and said "thank you" more often. Because a thank-you is a smile we can all see through our masks. Gratitude lights up our faces and ignites our spirits. It is a gift to help a hurting world.

THE PARENT TRAP

LIZ ALTERMAN

"Do you really believe indoor dining is increasing the spread?" my mother asked one winter afternoon as the pandemic continued to ravage our home state of New Jersey.

Calling from a booth inside Red Lobster, she sounded irked that COVID was once again ruining her plans. "I'm supposed to meet Johanna at Olive Garden on Thursday, and I'd hate to cancel."

I wished this conversation was a one-off. It wasn't. Since the start of the pandemic, my parents, both in their late 70s, neither in great health, had been brazenly cavalier. At the onset, my brothers and I offered to get their groceries and run their errands for them.

"That won't be necessary," my father assured us.

My siblings and I mistakenly assumed our parents would work their way through their packed freezer and pantry (where certain canned soups were older than a few of their grandchildren), and then place delivery orders. That wasn't the case.

My mother, undaunted by statistics and the stern warnings of Dr. Fauci, set off each day to make all her usual visits—church, the grocery store, friends' homes.

"Are you watching the news?" I asked repeatedly. "Have you seen the death toll? I'm not trying to scare you, but it's hitting people in your age bracket hardest. I want you to be safe —to take this seriously."

"I know, dear," my mother responded, "but your father and I aren't going to live forever."

My dad, chiming in on the extension, added, "We could be hit and killed by a bus tomorrow."

"Not if you stay inside your home," I said through gritted teeth.

COVID hastened that inevitable role reversal, the old switcheroo where the child becomes the parent. I found myself pleading with my mother as if she were a toddler, "Please don't touch your face! Don't put your hands in your mouth! Do you have your mask with you? Do you keep an extra in case you lose that one?"

"Oh honey, I'm being safe. You don't need to worry," she chuckled.

Hadn't I said the same thing to her during my college days moments before heading to a raucous house party where kegs and joints outnumbered attendees?

And yet I shouldn't have been surprised my parents were behaving this way. They'd long been guided by their peculiar inner compasses. Some of my earliest memories involved my father striding into the stockroom of Sears to fetch cases of motor oil when no sales associates were available to assist him. I could recall my mother, eight months pregnant with my youngest brother, making sandwiches for us in a supermarket parking lot when she was so ravenous she couldn't wait until we got home to eat. Pulling beach chairs out of the back of our paneled wagon, she told us we were having a picnic as fellow shoppers stared wide-eyed at our small circle as we devoured bologna and liverwurst inches above asphalt.

When I texted with my cousins or Zoomed with friends, they'd ask with concern, "How are your parents?"

How could I respond? *They are crazy. They are reckless. They are exactly the same as they've always been.*

Many of my friends have lost their parents to disease and old age. I couldn't answer them honestly, complaining that my parents' indifference to COVID kept me up at night, that I had visions of them intubated, dying alone because my mother insisted on going to Costco in search of the meatiest rotisserie chicken.

"They're hanging in there. Thanks for asking," was the best I could do.

———

"WHAT'S WRONG WITH THEM? Why won't they stay home?" my oldest son, Sam, asked.

He wanted his grandparents to remain safe and healthy; he also yearned for life to return to "normal" as quickly as possible. Eighteen and bound for his freshman year of college when the pandemic began, Sam knew all about staying home.

When faced with only online classes, limited activities, and countless dorm restrictions, he opted to take a gap year. As months passed, isolation and a steady stream of news about second waves and new strains left him wondering if "normal" was a thing of the past. *Would he get to cheer for his favorite baseball team or see a concert in person again?* he wondered aloud at breakfast, lunch, and dinner.

My teen felt as if his life was just beginning when it was put on hiatus by a virus that baffled scientists and incited conspiracy theorists. His disappointment and anxiety spiked alongside the number of positive cases.

In the sandwich generation cliché, I became the wilted

lettuce. I didn't know how to instill fear in my parents nor ease the worry of my son—and I was exhausted from trying and failing at both.

TWELVE-HUNDRED MILES AWAY IN FLORIDA, my in-laws, in their late 80s, have been holed up in their two-bedroom ranch for 14 months. They've taken no chances. When my sister-in-law visited, she sat on the other side of a screen door, six feet away, masked. My perennially good-natured father-in-law only once lamented missing the taste of his favorite beer when concern for his health prevented him from visiting his local wine shop.

We haven't seen them in more than a year, and on nights when worry keeps me awake until birds signal the dawn of a new day, I have wondered if we will ever see them again.

AT ANY AGE, every year of your life counts, but when you don't know how many you have left, you want to make the most of each one.

My mother wants to live as she always has, eating the sandwich when she feels like it rather than waiting. Over the past few years, she lost her sister and several of her closest friends. She is keenly aware that more time is never guaranteed.

My in-laws want to safeguard today so they can enjoy tomorrow.

My son wants it all.

I can't argue with any of them. The pandemic has shown me how little control any of us has. I can't force a strong-willed woman to stay home. I can't convince my teen that watching a

Mets game on television is just as good as catching it at Citi-Field. I can't promise my in-laws that they'll be able to return to their favorite activities—attending a symphony performance or tucking into a pastrami sandwich in a bustling deli—in the carefree way they once did, despite their endless patience.

When faced with the many challenges the pandemic has presented in my mid-life, caring for my nonchalant parents, concerned about my faraway in-laws, and helping my teen to navigate his new reality, the best I can do is try to let go of the constant worry. When my mom tells me she's venturing out to use her Kohl's Cash before it expires, I can roll my eyes but save my breath. When I Zoom with my in-laws, I can reassure them that we will visit as soon as it's safe. When my son asks if I think his college experience this fall will be "normal," I tell him that whatever it is, I'm sure he'll make the best of it.

And at times, I found that I've had to parent myself—giving my mind and body a much-needed time-out. When everything feels like too much, I walk through the woods and notice all the magical things that are just as they always were—the warm sun, the robins flitting overhead, the river rushing toward a greater opening. I take a deep breath and feel gratitude for all we still have.

The greatest lesson the pandemic has taught me is that each moment is too precious to waste.

WHO'S IN CHARGE HERE?

CORA WARING

During 2020's pandemic spring and summer, I hid from my husband and three children in my basement, consuming pep talks out of strangers' mouths: phrases like *you can do it* and *one more round,* which were equal parts banal and necessary. The nation's lack of top-down leadership regarding the coronavirus had left me flailing, so I let virtual fitness instructors bark out the next tiny segment of my life and felt better.

During the spring, I felt helpless. My almost-teenager wept for her friends, suffering reverse FOMO (there was nothing to miss out on), while my introverted youngest child celebrated the demise of physical school. My fourth-grade son played too much eyeball-searing *Fortnite,* and I compared the game's endless violence to the deaths happening just outside—lives obliterated with precision for being old, frail, or Black.

COVID forced my family to acknowledge our deep reliance on each other. Then we hated this dependency with increasing intensity. As the wife and mother, I scrambled for some compass to guide us through the new uncertainties but came up empty. Pre-COVID, my role was to absorb and nurture and fix. During

COVID, I felt only an internal splintering as my family vomited months of copious and erratic emotions at me with *Exorcist*-like precision.

In the basement though, I persevered. I rode my crappy stationary bike secure in the knowledge that my spandex-clad instructor would never forsake me. When she requested presence, I gave it, believing I could earn the ultimate reward of *later*. *Later*, when we'd leave our homes, unmasked. *Later*, when I'd recognize my family.

Our privilege was not lost on me. My husband's job continued to pay our mortgage. He worked from home now, and at first, this was a joy. But soon I grew bitter about all the hours he hid, employing his office door like a drawbridge and moat, while the children interrupted me constantly. In the evenings, I'd look at the clock accusingly when he finally appeared.

In the basement though, I waited on no one. My virtual fitness instructors all waited on me. I played the field, ghosting one instructor for another, or ditching the apps for YouTube. I extended my sessions, left the bike for the exercise mat, and learned how to do a Turkish get-up. *I'll do whatever you ask*, I breathed at my phone screen. *Just don't stop talking.*

I needed a Voice, an all-knowing entity to rely on through the uncertainty. Some people call this God, but mine went by many names—Ally and Tracy and Maddie and Nicole—all of whom sounded so convinced of my ability to do hard things, I couldn't help but want to please them. I wore their words like a chest plate of armor when I headed back upstairs to whatever battles awaited in my home.

Because after my precious basement time, I could better endure my son's meltdown at having to freewrite for ten minutes. I could allow myself grace when so many of my creative endeavors were rejected. I could try again because the Voice said I was worthy.

My time spent with the virtual fitness instructors felt like worship. It wasn't the exercise, though I'm sure the endorphins played their role. I was like an alcoholic embracing AA, a Catholic petting the rosary in her handbag, a person choosing a cigarette over a donut. None of these choices are necessarily healthy, but rather crucial, a prescribed way to respond to calamity and move forward. *Just give Mommy an hour in the basement!*

Before the world paused for contagion, I taught indoor cycling at a big box gym. I relished the opportunity to encourage 40 others, but none of the scripted motivation I used to shout translated as self-talk. I needed outside guidance to quell the demons of doubt murmuring in my brain. I'd text with a neighbor who'd asked how we were and answer, *Oh, you know, we're homebodies living our best life.* Then I'd call myself a liar.

I knew that the classes I engaged with were pre-recorded, that no virtual instructor truly saw me or the turmoil I carried into the basement each day. But they were a safe connection to the outer world when the rest of it was off-limits and terrifying.

Long ago, a man credited me with changing his life. He'd shown up at my gym a few months prior, wanting to regain control after a job loss, divorce, and weight gain. I prescribed three cycle classes a week and told him he could do it. Months later, he found me after class, down thirty pounds, with a new job and a hot, Brazilian girlfriend (his words). He thanked me for changing his life. *I didn't*, I told him. *You did.*

But years later, in the basement during a pandemic, I understood. Logging on, I felt the tingly embrace of a thousand phantom limbs. At reminders for gratitude, I cried, overcome by the luxury of what I had: a body and mind to perform hard work, an internet connection, my family's health. For the many negatives that felt compounded in quarantine, I could finally identify some positives too. My time with the virtual fitness instructors was like hitting refresh, enabling me to lead my family for another 24 uncertain hours, after which I could descend the stairs for another fix. Then, I went back up to find my children. I tried again.

MEMES, DREAMS, AND AUTOMOBILES

AMY HEINZ

We roll up to the last house and kid number five awkwardly climbs over the other man-children to the back row—the price he pays for living closest to the field. He doesn't miss a beat, dropping a wisecrack into the conversation, a clear sign these thirteen-year-olds have been perfecting their banter since kindergarten. It isn't lost on me that if the DMV really wanted to prepare me for driving under extreme conditions, they would have pumped a lethal combination of dirty cleats, armpits that matured faster than deodorant could become habitual, and goldfish cracker dust into the car during my driver's test all those decades ago.

"Yes!" shouts the alpha of the group.

The chatter immediately halts, and my son adjusts the volume on the stereo. Unabashedly off-key notes fill the air as all five boys join in an overly confident chorus. These Silicon Valley kids may spend a whole lot more time in freeway traffic than on backroad highways, but somehow they know—they *feel* —every single word of their baseball team's unofficial anthem, "God's Country."

With seconds to spare, we pull into the parking lot. The kids shuffle out, leaving behind empty protein bar wrappers, disheveled seatbelts, and a treasured memory I carry home with me through twilight traffic.

FOR YEARS, this was the rhythm of my life as the mom of three school-age children. Pick up, drop off, repeat. Pick up, drop off, repeat. Pick up, drop off, repeat. Until suddenly, it wasn't.

My well-traveled minivan—the one that looks like it's spent the better part of the last four years wearing a "kick me" sign—sat idle in our driveway for close to a month. When the time came to venture out, I cautiously returned to my throne. Instead of impatiently shouting my typical, "Did you remember to grab...?" over chaotic bodies piling in, I did my own slow checklist in eerie silence.

Bandana. Check. Winter gloves. Check. Hand sanitizer. Check.

My windshield wiper fluid had its work cut out for it. Not that the thick streaks of dust were interfering with my visibility. There was nothing to see. No unruly teenagers weaving in and out of the bike lane. No cars filled with party-ready balloons pulling into the park down the street. The only thing I had to be wary of at that moment was the unknown of an invisible, all-consuming virus.

As I rounded the first corner, I heard it. Clink. A distinct, familiar sound punched me in the gut. Another turn. Clink. And I was undone. A long-lost water bottle rolled around the backseat, like a tumbleweed on the open road. Where there had once been life, there was now an endless stretch of nothing.

I continued down barren streets on my brave quest for sustenance to feed the bottomless beasts now caged in my home, shifting awkwardly, a trespasser in my own space. It felt like just yesterday, and also lifetimes ago, that, just for fun, I had reset the odometer so my kids and I could play a game. I won, of course. In less than three days I had over 100 miles under my slowly fraying seat belt.

Given I clocked the triple digits without venturing beyond the five-mile radius of our small-ish town, the number seemed outrageous to my kids. It's like they didn't even know me. How many times had I bemoaned their demanding schedules? Proclaimed that my under-exercised glutes might be permanently melded into that off-brownish leather? No wonder I never seemed to accomplish anything, I would joke. But there was always an edge to my voice.

So this shift to being home and not juggling schedules should have been a welcome one. Without the burden of practices, playdates, volunteer commitments, and the adorably adorned aisles of Target's seasonal items pulling me in with their siren song, just imagine who I could be. What I could accomplish. This was my chance to trade in my steering wheel for a blank canvas. Time was on my side.

As luck would have it, I was immediately thrown into a few positions that were definitely not sought-after, redefining roles. A fifth-grade math tutor. A professional organizer. A puzzler. A constant ray of sunshine in the eye of a hurricane. A serial disappointer. A risk-assessment manager. And that's just to name a few. These gave me a chance to discover what I did *not* want to be.

None of the new opportunities presented helped me find my great undiscovered, world-class self. Instead, I found myself being swallowed whole. All those complaints of blending into the background in the Before Days? That was amateur hour.

Haphazardly arranged desk stations popped up on tables, countertops, and bedroom floors at a rate outnumbering the children now being schooled in the house. My quiet home office had been turned into an international business hub overnight. Everywhere I looked there were all kinds of crafts (not mine), laundry and dish piles (not mine), and demands (also, not mine).

"I hate fractions!"

"Is the internet working for you?"

"Get out! Get out! Get out! Mooo-ooom! He won't get out of my room!"

"Can we have something that's actually good for dinner tonight?"

The constant realities and demands of pandemic life on my ever-present family were unrelenting. Not only had this shelter-in-place booted me from the literal driver's seat, but also the metaphorical one.

I often found myself begging the universe for a moment of ever-loving silence. I'd happen upon it in a chaos-free closet or another solo lap around the block. All too often, though, it was waiting for me in the kitchen pantry. That's the spot where, sneaking a bite of some random piece of chocolate my middle son had miraculously overlooked, enjoying a beautiful moment of solitude, the irony hit me.

I *had* rediscovered who I was while stuck in this house. I was lonely. And I wasn't at all alone in my loneliness. There were four other people in this house. Four people I adore spending every waking minute with. But somehow, we were each equally together and desperately alone.

I missed being out in the world among familiar roads, faces, sounds, places.

I missed my one-on-one chlorine-scented conversations with my little swimmer girl. I missed exchanging "Hellos" with my kids' former teachers on my way to edit heartfelt, unintention-ally hilarious fourth-grade opinion essays. I missed cheering—or, somedays, cringing—alongside friends in metal bleachers, throwing cash and art supplies at non-uniformed siblings so they would feed and entertain themselves over the next few hours, while we casually gossiped, pretending we didn't know exactly what the score was and what needed to happen the next time our own kid came to the plate.

I missed our five-mile radius and all the people and places it held tight.

Over the next few weeks, it became clear that I wasn't the only one feeling this way. People started to creep back in. Most definitely not through our front door—or even the sliding door of my minivan. But there they were.

Text strings lit up my phone filled with hilarious memes. Next came outrageous tales of horror scenes taking place inside perfectly landscaped homes. Calendar reminders popped up that it was Zoom trivia night with one of my kid's friends and their moms. Sweats, slippers, and BYOB mugs started showing up at six-ish-foot intervals in dimly lit backyards.

Whispers filled patios late into the night. Without the ache of high heels or the struggle of strapless bras, there was no reason not to stick around . . . just a little while longer. We humbly admitted to missing simple things like carpool conversations and the insights they provided into our children's worlds. We declared there were some things we'd never do again, like spending another Saturday night wearing clothes that pinched in odd places to impress people we hadn't even thought about in months. We vented about how our sisters, fathers, and kids' friends' parents were making us crazy with how strict—or lenient—they were being in the middle of this soul-sucking pandemic. How we'd never, ever Zoom again, except for maybe to have college reunions every five months instead of five years. We reassured unnerved friends that our bathrooms were scrubbed and sprayed, our hand sanitizer was free-flowing, and that someone's holiday road trip—no stops!—to visit their isolated parents, maybe, probably wasn't the greatest crime against humanity.

In the unapologetic laughter and debate, I started to reclaim the "me" I thought I'd lost somewhere along the way. I was reminded of what I stood for, as well as what I wouldn't fall for. While I'd always had shared experiences with these friends, the intensity of a pandemic shifted the focus from our children's needs to our human connections. Together we grieved our families' collective losses. We started feeling less alone, and more seen.

I got antsy to rediscover myself all over again. Not in silent, solitary days at home—which will eventually materialize and I'll surely lament they came all too soon— but back there in the nitty-gritty ordinariness of a busy life. It was there, in my pre-pandemic days, that I'd created these deeply woven connections alongside three growing, dynamic little humans. Big and little victories, heartbreaking defeats, budding independence, surprising creativity, and unexpected friendships were not in spite of, but because of, the many hours I'd spent sitting in school auditoriums, itty-bitty classroom chairs, baseball bleachers, and, yes, even that dirty minivan driver's seat.

This morning looks like a typical Saturday in March, but it feels monumental. Today marks an entire year since life harshly and abruptly stopped. I load the trunk with a folding chair, snacks, and blankets, glancing at my watch. Just a week into daylight savings time, 6:40 a.m. feels notably chilly and dark. I climb in, starting the engine to warm the car. My twelve-year-old hops into the passenger seat without a word. This morning there's no grumbling about waking up so early. He hasn't thrown a single fit complaining that his socks are so, so itchy. And the hour drive we have in front of us seems like a small price to pay to get to a field someone has allowed his team to use for their first scrimmage in 15 disheartening months.

I sip warm coffee out of my wine-stained travel mug. One of my favorite songs comes on the radio, and there's a humming coming from my frustratingly silent kid. I can't help but smile.

As I glance in his direction, my breath catches a little. Just out his window, to the east, there's a beautiful sunrise, and the water of the San Francisco Bay sparkles. There's no question, a new day is dawning. On the horizon, and in us too. We've still got a ways to go, but we're coming back to life. Together.

I loosen my grip on the steering wheel and make myself right at home. The mud-streaked view from the driver's seat is pretty damn great, after all.

ACKNOWLEDGMENTS

We are grateful to our families, for once again being patient with us during this book publication process.

We would like to thank Autumn Purdy, for her editorial help. You are such a valuable member of our community. We are so lucky to have you.

We'd also like to thank Meg Reid, our cover designer, for once again producing a design that matches our vision for our book.

We could not have even considered this project without the input of our HerStories community. You shared your experiences — by submitting your stories and completing our survey — as well as your ideas for the focus of this project.

We would especially like to thank our writing groups, such as the amazing women of the Small Steps groups, for being an inspiration and support to us as we tried out new ideas and ways to connect with our community.

ABOUT THE CONTRIBUTORS

Elizabeth Suarez Aguerre is a teacher, writer, mother, wife, and beach bum. She is the author of nine educational books, is one of the featured women writers in the anthology *The HerStories Project: Women Explore the Joy, Pain, and Power of Female Friendship*, and has been a featured voice on Mamapedia. She expresses her passionate opinions and shares her random musings on her blog: But Then I Had Kids.

Liz Alterman is the author of a young adult thriller, *He'll Be Waiting*. Her memoir, *Sad Sacked*, chronicling her and her husband's simultaneous unemployment, will be released by Audible Originals in late 2021. She lives in New Jersey with her husband, three sons, and two cats, and can be found microwaving the same cup of coffee all day long.

Rebecca Atkinson is a 40-year-old cis woman living with her children and partner in Bradford, England. She works as a journalist in the cultural sector and is currently writing the first draft of her second novel about a young woman who is sent a treasure map by her errant father. During the pandemic, she formed a new writers' circle focused on self-care and mutual support—something she didn't realise she needed until it came along. She loves to write about the sea, despite living a long way from the coast.

Caroline Berger is a writer, editor, digital content guru, and activist based in Baltimore. Her writing has been published in such literary journals as *Flaneur Foundry, La Petite Zine, Pindeldyboz, Barrow Street,* and *Vibrant Gray.* She is a digital marketing specialist for LifeBridge Health, where she focuses mostly on the comprehensive violence prevention and intervention work of the Center for Hope.

Kimi Ceridon is a freelance writer and essayist in Medford, MA. She has masters' degrees in Mechanical Engineering from MIT and Food Studies from Boston University. Her personal essays are featured in *Dreamers Creative Writing, HerStry, For Women Who Roar* and *Snapdragon.*

Joan Delcoco is a brain injury survivor who writes to retrain her brain, make sense of the world, and connect with others. In previous lives, she has been a grant writer for nonprofit organizations, a stay-at-home mother to two now-grown children, and a middle school English teacher. She lives in Northern Virginia with her husband and daughter.

Laurie Foos is the author of the novels *Ex Utero* and *The Blue Girl,* among others, as well as the novellas *The Giant Baby* and *Toast,* and her short fiction has appeared in *Solstice: A Magazine of Diverse Voices, Quarterly West,* as well as in the anthologies, *Wreckage of Reason: XXperimental Women Writing in the 21st Century,* and *Chick-Lit: Postfeminist Fiction* . Her nonfiction has appeared in *Brain,Child, Motherwell,* and in the anthologies *At the End of Life: True Stories About How We Die* and *So Glad They Told Me: Women Get Real About Motherhood.* She teaches at Goddard College and Lesley University and lives on Long Island with her two kids.

Ellyn Gelman is a storyteller by nature. After raising three children she earned an MFA in creative writing and relocated to Manhattan. She teaches creative writing at Westport Writers Workshop in CT. She loves to visit National Parks. Her best adventures include dogsledding in Alaska and white water rafting down the Rio Grande.

Caroline M. Grant is co-director of the Sustainable Arts Foundation. She served on the editorial board of Literary Mama for ten years, including five as editor-in-chief. She has published essays in *The New York Times, Washington Post, Salon, Ozy,* and a number of other outlets, and has also co-edited two anthologies: *Mama, PhD* and *The Cassoulet Saved Our Marriage.* She lives in San Francisco with her husband and two sons.

Lea Grover is a writer and speaker in Chicagoland, living with her Platonic Parenting Partner, four children, five cats, and the enthusiastically supportive ghost of her late husband. When not completely lost in her own house and head, she can be found painting, cooking, or plotting yet another unfinished book.

Amy Heinz is a freelance copywriter and parenting writer living in the San Francisco Bay Area with her husband and three children. Her work—which receives glowing reviews from her mother—can be found on *Huffington Post, Scary Mommy, Disney Baby, Pop Sugar,* and her neglected parenting blog, Using Our Words. When she's not driving her kids to places where she cheers too loudly, she's planning her next escape to the beach.

Writing has been **Laurel K. Hilton**'s passion as long as she can remember. She is an author, writing coach, and social historian. Laurel has been featured in four anthology collections, performed her work on the radio, and co-produced the highly acclaimed stage show *Listen to Your Mother–San Francisco*. She and her husband, daughters, and Aussie cattle dog crew live in the San Francisco/Bay Area.

Marie Holmes has written for *Good Housekeeping, Cosmopolitan*, the *Washington Post*, and other publications. She has received awards from Gival Press, the Bronx Writers Center, and the Center for Fiction. She lives in New York City with her wife and their two children.

Jennifer Lang is forever a mutt: born in Berkeley, sleepless in Tel Aviv. Pushcart Prize and Best American Essays nominee. Flash nonfiction in *Midland Journal, Bending Genres, The Gravity of The Thing, Atticus Review, CHEAP POP, Pithead Chapel, Citron Review*, and elsewhere. Findable at a desk or on a yoga mat and at israelwriterstudio.com,

Kimberly Hensle Lowrance has been a nonprofit director, consultant, blogger, community volunteer, and elected official. She's also a writer who has been published in the *Boston Globe, Embark Literary Journal*, and *Mothers Always Write*, among other outlets. She is currently at work on her first novel. Additionally, Kimberly is a producer and on-air host for A Mighty Blaze, an organization of writers and creatives who love books, authors, and bookstores and who work to bring attention to these essential parts of our culture during COVID-19 and beyond.

Leslie Mac is a Brooklyn girl, organizer, and communications expert. She currently serves as the Communications Director for The Frontline. A seasoned Digital Strategist & Social Media Advisor, she founded LM Consulting to help her clients create diverse, imaginative campaigns and branding that focus on inclusivity and justice-minded content. Recent clients include Google, UltraViolet, Articulate, UMass Amherst, Amazon, Meadville Lombard Theological School, Canvas8, and The Advancement Project.

Gretchen M. Michelfeld's essays have appeared in *The Washington Post, Motherwell, Parents.com, Good Men Project, Natural Selections*, and *Real Simple*. Her award-winning film, *As Good As You*, is available on EPIX, iTunes, and Prime. She has a BA from Vassar College, an MFA from Sarah Lawrence, and she lives with her family in Jackson Heights, Queens.

Jenny Moore writes and edits fiction and nonfiction. Her writing has appeared in several anthologies, most recently *This Is What America Looks Like*. She is currently finishing a novel.

Tabitha Nordby is a freelance writer who lives in Winnipeg, Canada with her partner and their three spoiled cats. Tabitha's work history includes being a terrible waitress, an average barista, a used bookseller, and most recently, a public librarian and a college educator. Tabitha's favorite activities include traveling, writing creative nonfiction, reading, and more traveling. Although traveling has not been an option for the last year-and-a-half, Tabitha hopes to do a second hike on the Camino de Santiago in Spain in 2022, which will certainly provide more opportunities for reading and writing.

Anne Pinkerton studied poetry at Hampshire College and received an MFA in creative nonfiction from Bay Path University. Her writing often circles around grief, loss, illness, and coping with these painful realities in our lives. She has been published in *Modern Loss, Hippocampus Magazine, Entropy, Ars Medica, Lunch Ticket, The Bark,* among others.

Autumn Purdy lives in Westerville, Ohio where she writes creative nonfiction and poetry, dabbles in nature photography, and serves as a book reviews editor for *Literary Mama.* Her work has been published by *HerKind Collective, The HerStories Project, Literary Mama, The Sunlight Press,* and *Sharing Magazine.* She's writing a memoir about her recurrent miscarriage experience and path to motherhood.

Jodie Sadowsky is a Connecticut lawyer turned freelance writer. She married her high school pro date (not that same night) and they're still growing (up) together as they raise their three children. Jodie's writing centers around her life's biggest roles: mother, daughter, partner, sister, friend. Some of her work has been published online at *The Kitchn, Kveller, Tablet* and *Cottage Life*; the rest exists on her laptop, her notebooks and in her head.

Natalie Serianni is a Seattle-based writer, instructor, and mother of two, whose writing has appeared at *Motherwell, The Manifest-Station, Literary Mama, SheKnows* and *Today's Parent.* She's at work on a memoir about motherless mothering.

Chanize Thorpe is a NY-based lifestyle editor and writer. A former Air Force dependent, she has spent over two decades traveling the world, contributing to both national and international publications as well as a variety of websites. Her work has appeared in outlets from *Brides Magazine* to Shondaland.com. She is the mother of two women and a proud member of the LGBQTIA+ community.

Cora Waring lives in Brookline, MA. Her work previously appears or is forthcoming in *Catapult, River Teeth's "Beautiful Things," Santa Clara Review, Train River,* and other publications. When she's not chasing after her three children, she teaches indoor cycling classes around Boston.

Andra Watkins is the author of four books. Her memoir *Not Without My Father: One Woman's 444-Mile Walk of the Natchez Trace* hit the *NYT* bestseller list in October 2015. Her well-reviewed Nowhere trilogy targets the fiction lover. She gives rousting keynote speeches and has yet to meet a destination she doesn't like.

A writer and storyteller from Burbank, CA, **Suzanne Weerts** is the Artistic Director for JAM Creative, a storytelling project committed to bringing diverse voices from the page to the stage while supporting local charities. You can read her essays in The Sun, Good Old Days magazine and on numerous parenting websites. A graduate of the University of North Carolina at Chapel Hill, Suzanne has raised hundreds of thousands of dollars for public school arts education and mental health programs while raising two compassionate, capable, decent democrats. Now an empty-nester, she has turned her attentions to raising her pandemic puppy and completing her memoir.

Shari Winslow is a high school English teacher who grew up in Montana and lives with her family near the shore of Puget Sound in Washington State. She never leaves the house without at least one notebook and something to read. Her work has previously appeared in *Whitefish Review, The Fourth River, Hipmamazine, Toasted Cheese, the Literary Kitchen,* and others.

Shannon Connor Winward is the author of *The Year of the Witch* (Sycorax Press, 2018) and *Undoing Winter* (Finishing Line Press, 2014, winner of the SFPA's Elgin Award for best speculative chapbook). Her work appears widely in places like *The Magazine of Fantasy & Science Fiction, Rivet, Analog, Lunch Ticket, Literary Mama, Pseudopod: Artemis Rising,* the *Minola* and other *Reviews* and, most recently *Deaf Poets Society, Skelos, Crow Toes Magazine,* and *Twilight Worlds:* a *Best of NewMyths* Anthology. She is the erstwhile recipient of eclectic honors including a Best of the Net nomination, runner-up in a Celtic ballad contest, and a fellowship in fiction for her home state of Delaware. Shannon lives in the brokedown tower of her body in a blue room, where she edits *Riddled with Arrows Literary Journal.*

Amber Wong is an environmental engineer in Seattle who writes about culture, identity, and her firsthand knowledge about risks posed by hazardous waste sites, although usually not all in the same essay. Recent work has been published in *Creative Nonfiction, Stanford Magazine, The Sunlight Press, Catamaran Literary Reader,* and *Tahoma Literary Review,* among others. Amber earned an MFA from Lesley University and is currently working on a memoir.

Marya Zilberberg came to the U.S. as a teen from what was then the Soviet Union, and now lives in the foothills of the Berkshire Mountains in Western Massachusetts. She is the author of *Between the Lines: Finding the Truth in Medical Literature*, a guide to evaluating medical evidence. Her work has appeared in *Salon, Tablet Magazine, Longreads, Massachusetts Review,* and *Hippocampus,* among others.

Jessica Smock is a writer, editor, and educational consultant. A graduate of Wesleyan University, she received her doctorate in educational policy in 2013. She lives with her husband, son, daughter, two dogs, cat, and parakeet in western New York State.

Stephanie Sprenger is a writer, editor, music therapist, and producer of Listen To Your Mother Boulder. Her work has been published in *O Magazine, The Washington Post, The Chicken Soup for the Soul* series, *Cosmopolitan.com, Redbook.com, Mutha Magazine,* and *Scary Mommy,* among other places. She lives with her husband, two daughters, and their beloved rescue dog in Colorado.

For my information on our contributors, visit: https://www.herstoriesproject.com/pandemic-midlife-crisis/

Made in the USA
Middletown, DE
29 December 2021

57263680R00129